# FINDING HONOR

## The Journey to Truth

## Christine Beckwith

20/20 Vision Press

Finding Honor/ Christine Beckwith, 20/20 Vision Press - 1st ed.

ISBN 978-1-954036-03-1

# Contents

*I dedicate this book to God and Jay Doran.*

*One sent the other to save me.*

# FOREWORD

*Les Brown*

Sharing your innermost intimate trials with the world through expression is a part of the healing process. Nighttime is the right time to reflect. Early mornings are the time to deflect. Life's journey affords us many obstacles. Every day our experiences provide us with an opportunity to make choices that are either correct or decisions we may regret.

Tears stream as part of the healing process and at what point do you honor yourself? Those we love also love us, but there are times in life when you have to be intentional about how to love yourself. Reflection and self-talk are one of those ways to make sure our mental wellness is not defeated.

Time and distance are a quiet reminder some things are better off not said. Being quiet and allowing yourself to feel and be present is hard work, but your genuine self is how you honor YOU!

Children are known for saying the darndest things and as we age this statement remains true. Today you choose you and no longer have unrealistic expectations from others. Triumph is our goal. Today is about honoring me, my goals, my priorities, and my vision for the remainder of my days on this earth.

God has manifested something great in all of us and sharing those gifts with others through written word is mastery.

YOU HAVE SOMETHING SPECIAL IN YOU!

~ Les Brown

# PREFACE

Writing this book was the most exciting accomplishment of my life and, surprisingly, led to a sad realization.

The most exciting because I realized, I am now a fully honest person and getting here was incredibly difficult.

The saddest because I am now of an age where I can see the end of my life ahead, albeit (hopefully) far off in the distance. Still, I know the sand of the hourglass is less than half full for me.

Both realizations occurred while authoring this book.

# CHAPTER 1

# A Time for Honor

There is a time for honor. A time for sin. A time to ask for forgiveness, to regret. A time for overcoming or shrinking, as well as growth and retribution. A time to advance and a time to retreat. Eventually, there comes a time to find honor. To honor thy self.

This time comes by listening to our internal wiring; the voice inside our souls, not the one in our heads that sabotages good thoughts, self-doubt, or self-pity. The voice inside our whole being which makes us sick to our stomach when we betray someone or something and riddles us with guilt when we lie. The voice that aches like we are dying when we hurt from heartbreak.

Honor comes with time after ignoring or depleting ourselves. Honor is a path we find on our way to salvation.

As I sit here writing my fifth book, but my second solo book, I have spent many years, in fact, decades, contemplating the lessons I possess in my mind that I yearn to share. I thought in this introductory chapter I would share the extensive list of titles I scratched onto my iPhone notes' section over an extended period as fleeting inspirational thoughts came and went. *Finding Honor* was the last and most recent one. But I digress and with the hope of using some of the titles in future books, I will keep the list secret.

*Finding Honor* is the story of a journey to honesty and is about honoring ourselves. This is something many of us do not do. Many of us die trying or detour down the wrong path in life, unable to find our way back. *Finding Honor* is a hard and long walk and our Journey to the Truth is equally as much work for most of us. Hearing the call to find honor and embark on a journey to truth is incredibly challenging work but worthy work, and work I hope will inspire those of you seeking a happier, healthier, and more meaningful existence.

God, I know, is who saved me when I was at my most dire despair and on my knees begging him to help me. He would not show up straight away; no, he let me suffer a good long time until I realized he was teaching me I had to save myself. I have spent much time talking to God in my lifetime. I believe most of us have an imaginary power we pray to whom we call God, and I believe in my heart that is who heard me on those wretched days. It is this steadfast belief system inside of me I credit for helping me ultimately rise.

I could not talk about my strife to many humans on this earth. I feared most would cast judgment or not truly help or understand me. I found the human I could talk to was Jay

Doran, CEO of Culture Matters, and my accidental friend and fellow philosopher. Jay showed up in my world to hear me lecture and I repaid the same debt of gratitude to attend one of his lectures. From this casual trigger, our Journey to the Truth began.

I have learned whatever we put our belief in will have an almighty power. God is a universal word and belief system all rolled into one. I salute all our Gods who come to save us in the dark, who help us not be alone in our heads, and who give us something to hold onto. I salute the Jay Dorans of the world who can listen and guide, who can theorize, and who can provide honest and often painful insight to help us course correct. Through Jay's mentorship I completed The Hero's Journey and the Liar Lid self-development processes which were long and painful journeys to shedding layers of protective walls I had built around a false narrative of my life. I mean, I am still, at my most raw and naked self, the same person I was within the confines of those walls; I simply now exist without those chains.

I am free now. And everything has changed.

# CHAPTER 2

# Premonitions and Recurring Dreams

I awoke startled. The room was lit by a hallway window, blocked by a wall in front of me. The light snuck in through two doors set far apart on either end of the facing wall. I was lying in the full-size bed I shared with my older sister. Also in our room were bunk beds I sometimes slept in with my baby sister, who had recently left a crib. The room in our trailer was slightly reconstructed by removing the wall between two rooms to create a large room where all three of us slept in one place. The girls' room.

Abruptly I sat up in bed. Again. Awake now and aware of yet another night where my dreams replayed as a movie stuck repeating the same scene.

I remembered my dream. My father was standing in the doorway of the lit hallway; the bedroom was dark, so the images of my mother and father standing at either door were vivid. On one end, my father, and on the other, my mother, and they were playing tug-o-war with a rope. My father, who has facial hair and freckles, had a plain face in my dream, and his skin was smooth, and the same color, but he was bald and had no freckles. On the other hand, my mother's face was charred as if burned. Her face, of course, in real life was a plain one, all one color with no hair or freckles. What did this mean? Why were they tugging at this rope? Why were their images skewed as I described? What was the meaning of this odd, recurring dream?

Even at the tender age of six or seven, I recall thinking there was a meaning behind the repeated dream. Today, 45 years later, I am still questioning it, still calling up its memory.

I dreamed this dream for four or five nights and then again, a few weeks later. Every time I awoke, startled, rubbing my eyes. I even tried to explain what was occurring to my parents, but they did not seem to believe me and discarded it at the time as embellished child talk. Still, I knew then, as I know now, there was something subconsciously driven in the image and the repetitive nature of its occurrence.

Over my entire life I have had this keen sense of self-analyzation tied to my psyche and even when I have been in perilous flight running from some emotion threatening to cripple me or drive me to dark places, my brain had a mind of its own.

I laugh at that statement because it is quite literally true for all of us. Our brains, an organ in our body that rules our thoughts and internal speak,It's has driven me on bad GPS to places I would later need to come save myself from. All human beings spend their lives trying to figure this out and I have spent a lifetime correcting course and then documenting, meticulously how I have overcome these spontaneous mindsets seeking to deter me. But I digress.

I have studied altruism and empathy like my life depended on it and in this book, I will dive into both mindsets because both are strengths and deterrents to success. I possess and have control of an extremely strong will in both areas. I have learned to use them like superpowers, but it is a double-edge sword which wielding successfully means mastering the edge that cuts and not the one that stands to slay you. It is a real trick to succeed in business, and life, if you have great empathy and do not know how to control its constant calling.

My recurring dreams would happen sometimes even during the day as if to teach me that I did not control the dream's content or timing. I also experienced both premonitions that would come true and reflection through metaphoric imagery that would provide insight and add great depth in my thinking. These insights would become my genius ability to navigate in business and life. I was not aware of this subconscious thinking for a long part of its existence; however, once I had my internal epiphany, it periodically became this angel appearing whenever I needed to either help or steer a new course. Its precision in directing me to incredible things and out of harm's way seems magical to me still to this day.

I would learn later in my life that my parents were going through something then. As a young child, I had an all-knowing sense of this personal strife, and today, as I write this, I do not know what was really happening, just a strong internal sense of strife, and when disharmony resolved, so did my reoccurring dreams. It was as if the ghost who came to haunt me found what it was looking for over time and simply departed never to be seen again.

I wish I could control the premonitions. But I cannot. I have an active mind and when I think about my life, I realize interesting reoccurring dreams, thoughts, and premonitions have spanned my entire life. Another occurred right after my great-grandmother died. My siblings were at the hospital when she passed. I had seen her the day prior. I knew she was near and I had said my peace and how much I loved her, but I was not there for her final moment which I regretted. I had a new job and felt the pressure to return to work.

My great-grandmother was an incredible person and human and I loved her with all my soul. Naturally, her death had a profound effect on me. Within a few weeks of her passing I was given a few mementos and keepsakes from her belongings. I have kept an old jewelry box filled with costume jewelry and an old dresser I believe once served as a make-up table. I recall a round powder puff container sitting on the dresser filled with this big powder duster. My great-grandmother Louise, who I am named after (my middle name), was a woman who cared about how she looked. She had little in the way of possessions, but she had some genuinely wonderful things. Her hair was always done, and I always recall her wearing jewelry and nice blouses.

One of her sons and my great uncle had given her a Bulova watch. I wore her watch when I received this jewelry box. Within a week or two of her passing, when I put that watch on and noticed it was broken and it did not keep time, I did not care. It reminded me of her and I decided I would wear it ornamentally and later I could have it fixed.

I found myself one afternoon laying on the couch. As I drifted off to sleep, I raised my arm behind my head and the 'ta tink, ta tink, ta tink' sound of a ticking timepiece sounded in my ear, startling me awake. As I thought about this and silently acknowledged the watched was working, I knew on a purely practical level there was a mechanical reason as to why it had begun working suddenly. But for me it was symbolic, and I chose to believe my great-grandmother was with me. I felt a closeness to her memory in every tick tock of that watch sounding off as if it were her heart beating in my ear.

That night as I lay in my bed preparing to sleep, I prayed to my God. I prayed to my great-grandmother, too. I told her I loved her and thanked her for all her stories and all the things I knew she had done in her life to bring joy to my own. I was a descendent of her body, her once egg bred into another life, who bred into a life that bred into mine. I was a clear extension of her. And then I fell asleep.

The next morning, I woke up with a vivid awareness I had been talking to my great-grandmother in my dreams. She had come to the side of my bed exactly where I was sleeping, and she sat, smiling down at me. We had our final talk. It felt real. I felt relieved. Even though I knew my mind was imagining this, I remember thinking how beautiful my brain had been to evoke such a tale in my mind during my subconscious awareness. What a wonderful gift! And how grateful I was for such a gift.

I have often thought the brain and the heart are at war: one directing our thoughts and one directing our feelings. Our feelings are a natural state of physical being, and our brain witnesses those feelings directing us towards or away from known logic. Yes, we are aware of good or bad, hurt or happiness, and we do know what burns us and what propels us. Because the heart cannot work alone, and neither can the brain.

The night my great-grandmother came to sit with me in my dreams, my brain and heart were working in tandem, on their own, while I slept to tell me a remarkable story of careful goodbyes. That night my body let me have closure and find happiness during a sad time in my life; my dreams allowed me to discover the missing piece life had not provided me. My dream of her visiting would re-occur for many nights until one day she simply stopped coming to visit me.

I had more dreams of visitors and more daydreams and premonitions over my life. Some were closing chapters in my life: a goodbye from a lifelong friend who passed, a daydream of a baby crying, a specific baby to whom I was not connected but whose parents I was close to, only to realize the baby had been crying at the same time as a scary incident later shared with me in an unreal, alarming, and startling discovery by both sides in a phone call leaving myself and them shook with the realization I had imagined from 1,000 miles away the very scene that was happening in real-time.

I know how this sounds and I realize this will be dismissed by some readers. All I can say is each of these stories are one hundred percent true and real. And all of it in reflection tells me I have had a real connection to emotion and people. And that distance, time, and logic are defied by the intensity of emotion. I have accepted this as a superpower I possess, I do not control, and one I cannot and would not want to manipulate. Rather, I choose to use this for good doing.

This superpower is at work every day now, in the rooms I sit in, when I speak to strangers and even when I read and watch interactions which are not one-on-one type connections. I am constantly feeling, and as such, exhausted every single night and wasted by the sheer physicality of having this level of reaction to my surroundings.

I have often felt misunderstood because these feelings can make people feel exposed, can hit people in a way that feels intrusive and, with especially awkward encounters, leave someone wondering how I could have guessed how they feel. And while I have accepted this is who I am, and this superpower is an embedded trait I cannot extinguish, I often wish I could turn it off.

Later in another chapter, I will speak to the turning-off factor I stumbled upon in a not-so-healthy way, as you might guess. And again, this is not unique to me but something I no longer try to reason or question. I have no idea how many others feel like me, are like me, or suffer like me with this hypersensitivity to my surroundings.

In ending on this topic, I believe in my premonitions and my visitors in my dreams as real signs with a sense of truth and meaning, and while I cannot predict when they will come or go, I will never disregard them. Even when someone denies something I suspect to be true, it always proves to be exactly as I sensed it was once unveiled. This is both a gift and a burden for me to bear. But so is life and so is love. Incredible gifts are often a burden. It is in finding the beauty in those gifts that you can tolerate its burden. Beauty has a price and so does life and love. A price everyone must shoulder to experience.

# CHAPTER 3

# Salvation

"His name is Tom not Tim," she said. I wondered why nobody for months had ever corrected me. During the time I knew Tim, I mean Tom, I must have called him by the wrong name dozens of times. I was embarrassed. I wish Tom himself had told me the very first time I misspoke. But here we were months down the road and Tom and I had built a relationship on falsehood, and it stung and made me scratch my head, too.

This correction was necessary, of course, as is constantly learning from those brave enough to tell us we are wrong when we are. Enter stage left those who choose to counsel or coach. People sometimes want information and sometimes not. Nobody really wants to hear the tough stuff. Twenty years ago, when I sought counseling for the first time, this was me; I wasn't open to hearing the tough stuff.

I had broken a great relationship; one where I loved the other individual deeply. It was inexplicable to me why my actions were driving me away from this person I had vowed to be loyal to. I had to find the answers so I could live with myself, so I could understand the reasons for my unexpected actions.

What would ensue from this query of my actions was a journey to the truth, hence the tagline of this book. I found and never expected to figure out this truth; it was both lifesaving and life-altering. I knew, deep in my secret mind, where ideas live, I never dared to say them out loud and still find shocking, once I put in the work and faced the honesty, the truths unearthed would be life-changing.

In some instances, these truths were earth-shattering realizations and made me quiver in the instant of facing facts about who I had become or was at that time. My journey would leave me forever evolved and purified in ways that would save me and eventually save the honor of my internal image as well.

In many ways, learning about who I was in a brutally honest way meant facing bad and selfish habits; behaviors I had been doing for decades, sometimes my entire life, causing harm both outwardly and inwardly, leaving a wake of destruction. It would take brave people I trusted to tell me what no one else dared say to me. And sometimes, the lessons came in even more destructive ways from catastrophes brought on by self-neglect or unintentional wrongdoing.

I mean, my story is not unique I know. I have made this promise to share my darkest hours and bring light and life to those times and moments in my life I thought I would forever leave buried. I choose to turn them into someone else's guidance; adversity avoidance or even devastation diverted.

I wish I could have seen the future or had someone warn me more strongly when I took dead-end roads. But I think I know as I write this, even if a hero of epic strengths and persuasion could have come into my story and stood before me preventing me somehow from going towards the danger, I would have fought that person to their death to find the path to destruction. The habits, actions, and practices we kill ourselves with, the vices and sins, distractions, and deceits, all blanketed under our own justification, are a fast track towards pain. A pain dangerously addictive and subversive. When you subconsciously kill yourself with slow but methodical daily strikes that keep you sinking into oblivion, there is truly only one person who can save you. There can only be one hero in your story and life and that is each of us finding the strength to correct course and battling our way back to the light. I know that sounds deep, but it is a fitting description.

I share my story in this book in the most vulnerable of ways. By going public, I pay homage in words to the pain I experienced alone over many days and nights. The pain tortured me, left me sick, exhausted, and wasted by its relentlessness. I felt generally hopeless and entirely desperate, even while living a public life portraying the exact opposite; all while smiling every day and pretending I had life figured out and knew what I was doing.

Does this sound familiar? I hope those of you seeking change and those of you who sought out this book to find your truth, you begin to see the work to find truth, while undoubtedly daunting, is invaluable, lifesaving work.

When I thought about my polished exterior and how poorly it reflected the terrible, heartbroken internal intersection I faced, I realized I saw my own hurt and pain as a weakness to be hidden. I feared knowledge of my pain would be seen as a deficiency. I feared if others knew my pain, I would be lesser in their eyes, and I definitely felt knowing of my struggle would hurt me at work.

As I reflected and became more aware, I questioned, "Was I a fraud to hide for so long?" I have examined this thought extensively and the answer is NO! And thank the Lord for this. I am grateful in all honesty with the truth I found. I have never said I was anything I was not or tried to pretend I was not what I truly was. I have, however, allowed my public image on social media to follow the inside lines of what the planned marketing intended to highlight or spotlight which was my expertise in my field.

And that standing alone did not tell my whole story. I feel good today about my books which are all self-help books, are personal portrayals of the truth; I speak to my wrongs and confess my truths. Often over recent years, dark quotes of personal sharing have been shown in posted quotes from my books, and I am certain many people have seen a peek into the tortured parts of my story. My words are now used to help pull others from the morass of their own despair.

And I assure you as easy as it is to write for me and very publicly point out I have done all this self-work, this did not happen in a moment's time or come to fruition like flipping on a light switch. No! In fact, even though I found writing as a cure for a deep flow of internal emotion as a child, I did not then understand it would be a life-long necessity and joy for me. I recall writing for hours on end as a young girl, understanding only that in putting words on paper, I found comfort.

Understanding of the additional benefits writing offers is knowledge I found as an adult. Writing, it is now fully understood, is foundational to our development. I have taken many writing courses, published four books, launched two industry e-magazines, and helped others take the critical walk towards journaling which I realize is step one in this cathartic process.

I am still expanding my understanding as a teacher what the written word and sharing written words can do for people. Recently, I brought my books into class and read pointed lessons from them in a way I hope helped me connect the student and the life-changing lesson. Through those readings and further discussion, I could see the mental lightbulbs flashing in the eyes of my audience as they related to the depth of the reading. It was not all internal strife; often, positive lessons, business lessons, life lessons, happy endings, and victorious jubilation and triumph ensued. Regardless of the lesson topic, the emotional and written connection stem from the spiritual place by which we are connected.

For me, the discovery of the benefits to writing far outweighed the prestige and limelight they would render. I find it beyond gratifying to know my stories and words, personal lessons and tribulations could change lives, and, in the process, I could create a legacy of work to leave behind of growing, great magnitude.

Adult writing would not come to me as easily as childhood writing or youthful writing. Well, let me rephrase. Writing has always come easy; writing about my feelings has not. And as I aged, the gravity and depths of my emotional pain became harder to portray or face in my writing.

Bridging the knowing and writing gap would come from prodding during the writing of *Wise Eyes: See Your Way to*

*Success*, by the book's editor Candy Zulkosky. I met this talented writing coach through a new acquaintance. While writing my first published book, she encouraged me to answer a question she suspected most people reading would ask, "What was it like working in a male-dominated field my whole career?"

I personally thought she was crazy to insist on this question being answered and explored for inclusion in the book, but over time and after following a suggestion to write privately about it, I unleashed an inner geyser of feelings which had clearly been kept locked up for most of my life. This step alone, which I fought vehemently in my own mind as well as vocally to her, once overcome, began both a journey to the truth and the release of it as well.

I did not use writing alone to redirect me from a life filled with ample and consistent sin. I sought counseling several times over my lifetime. Talking to someone seemed to be the cure for the inexplicable thoughts my over-active mind could not stop.

I remember my first visit to a counselor. At first, I did not think talking to a stranger would work. After spotting a box of tissues in the room, I asked the therapist, "People come in here and cry to you?" The yes answer mocked me minutes later as I used the very same tissues.

My first therapist would not be the one for me. I went expecting answers and instead I received a head shaking affirmation of listening but no answers. I often left feeling unsatisfied although lighter for having unloaded my pain.

More than once I sought counseling to deal with confusing and conflictive internal thoughts.

It took 15 years from my first attempt, but eventually, I found my long-term counselor. This time I was bold enough and desperate enough to ask, "How does this work?"

My new counselor shared her belief system, her stance on guiding people and yes, an affirmation counseling was not about providing answers to questions per se but helping find a better understanding of what and why behind how we felt.

That is when it clicked for me. An epiphany. Much time and pain had passed with much misunderstanding of myself.

To be honest, I had not consistently counseled. I had tried and disliked it, then stopped only to return years later as if I knew there was more to do than feel unsatisfied, and then stop again for many years.

This time was different, and I knew immediately this time it would work. I trusted the person I was speaking to, and I learned this was key. In her eyes I saw empathy. In her antics I saw acknowledgement.

I spoke of my faith and at times the level of my raw pain I am certain could be felt by her as she winced or even welled up in the moment. Nonetheless, I felt like I was safe. And I can add here this realization also made me aware of who I could not work with. Whether I was talking to a boss, or a friend, or another, and I was standing in their judgement, I could not be open.

Not being open meant the effect desired and the depth needed could not be reached. Being open helped me stop being a walking wounded and helped me start being concise in my approach to seeking mental examination and leading me to the ultimate breakthrough to forever change my life. And now, this will forever change the lives of others who are on the same path looking, searching, and seeking their own truth.

This became decades of self-work put in consistently and permanently as a staple of my mental health. I am no longer afraid to speak this truth. I am no longer afraid to write this truth. This path will lead me to salvation.

# CHAPTER 4

# Knock, Knock!
# Who is There?

Therapy alone did not bring me to where I am today. The combination of trained psychological guidance, and the happenstance of meeting Jay Doran when I was working in and around the Philadelphia area proved to be magic for me. I thought I had my bases covered at the time, so I was not intentionally seeking advice. The depths of conversation when I spoke and interacted with Jay, became absolutely mind blowing for me.

In our ongoing interactions, we always found our way to a deep and philosophical discussion on various topics. We would go down rabbit holes, perplexed by the inequities and conundrums of life, much to our pleasure. Conversation often spanned extensive time. We would find keeping track of minutes to be elusive and look up to realize we sat in empty restaurants where all the patrons had left, and an anxious wait staff stood by waiting for us to pay our check. Our meeting was not a romance between a man and a woman. Still, in the knowledge of the language being romantic, there was the dance of two souls exchanging their mindsets and innermost opinions and feelings.

At the same time, Jay was often startling and offensive to me. I would go so far as to say I wondered if he would drop a bomb in our conversation for the sole purpose of being dramatic to manipulate or cause an effect in my response. But as time wore on, I learned the cadence of his thinking, his mannerisms, and his thought process—as best you can learn this from an acknowledged genius and modern-day philosopher. I knew every word Jay spoke he meant and every word Jay said came easily to him.

Yet his words were tied to a string of forethought and once explained, would lead you to examine the depths of behavioral science, then suddenly you realize somebody WAS smart enough to carry on a discussion leading to both truths and realizations.

As time passed, and Jay and my relationship naturally and organically grew into one of a student (me) and coach (him), we were often conflicted in our discussions. I denied with angry vigor the labeling of my personality in his first assessment, using words I considered negative to describe my traits. In this way, he uncovered blind spots I never knew or saw in myself. Instantly, I knew I would change by merely acknowledging these deficits, and my ego would no longer allow me to be egotistical. The irony was incalculable.

It occurs to me as I write, this process has been a consistent and ongoing continuum for over five years. Incredible truths have been discovered, in which no posturing would occur from my usual alpha. Repeatedly we landed in a place of exchange where I fell in line with his incredible brilliance, understanding of the human mind and its behavior, famous philosophers, and personal journeys. He and I have been and are still on a fantastic journey to the truth.

Jay Doran is still magical for me. I feel as if I sat and rubbed a stone long enough for a magic genie to appear. By talking with Jay, I have morphed and had epiphanies surface and life-changing thoughts altered. Each time a better, more morally aligned version of me emerges.

After being stuck in the quicksand earlier in my life, the combination of counseling and coaching I received proved to be the cocktail I needed to pull myself out finally. Today I am standing on the sidelines viewing the reflection, in wonderment and amazement, learning and living the lessons I have finally been taught.

I would add all of this occurred during a fragile mental time for me whilst I sought to fill a cavernous void and save myself from my internal image of worthlessness caused by callously and mistakenly choosing selfish and hurtful paths to feed an attention addiction. I barely recognize that person anymore; in my self-reflection and memory, she is all but dead.

Let us dissect the lessons I hope this book will help teach others who are lost. Others who are ready for the rebirthing of themselves. Others who need to save themselves from dying a slow but eventual death brought on by mental anguish and typically at their own hand.

I also know not everyone is trying to find their way to honor; many are happy being dishonest and cheating the system.

Many lack a conscious self-awareness and are happy being thieves and crooks, beggars and bastards, bitches, and boobs. Many do not attempt or ever arrive in a place to comprehend the recipe of failure they concocted. Many fail to acknowledge their role in creating and continuing a life landing them in bad luck spots and dead-end roads. I think many people repeatedly march down those roads, never recognizing they are on an inefficient hamster wheel of misfortune

For all of us living amongst these types of people, it is exhausting work trying to save them. We watch. We observe the ignorance, self-destruction, and misused resources. We question our wasted efforts to help. It is the fool's errand to try to help a lost soul who is unaware.

Or is it? Doing so is truly the question of humanity. Those who will save themselves and those of us who will help save others. Which one are you? In my lifetime, I have been both.

Whose door are you knocking on? And who is knocking on your door? That is the riddle.

Are you listening? Is anyone home to open the door? It is the most significant question of your life, and it needs answering. Every daycare worker, teacher, leader, parent, counselor, coach, doctor and nurse, firefighter and police officer, military man and woman are working to help save others. They are knocking on your door; are you listening? Is anyone at home?

Children follow their teacher's lessons without question. They submit to the discipline; all of us will. We crave it. Deep down we are wired to be led by strong leaders and we are attracted to them. Why? Because we believe they know the way. Because we want to follow someone who knows the way.

As we grow, we may tire of the accountability, and desire autonomy, or we turn into the teacher. Like I did. I became the leader in and of my life. I became the person who knows the way, who found the way by assessing my steps and my success.

The gap between learning and knowing can be long. I ask you, when think of your life are you learning and seeking answers about your own happiness and life journey? Are you troubled by the path you find yourself on? Are you wishing your life to be different?

If your answer to these questions rings true, ahead in these pages you will find guidance. Look to the self-quizzes designed to lead you to the inevitable answer you seek.

I hope if you are the teacher, you can ASK the right questions of others to help them find their truths, like Jay did with me, and like my counselors listened and questioned, allowing me to find the truths leading to honor.

*CHAPTER 5*

# Hardwired to Sin

If you have ever read the Bible, then you already know we were all born sinners. If you have not ever read the Bible, then you should know the statement is absolutely true.

We are hardwired to sin and migrate to paths and actions that are not good for us. Why is this? It is the fight between our physical attractions, the animal inside us, and a purer version of ourselves we eventually desire and become. It is also a matter of maturing to live according to the correct internal barometer.

I say this and recognize the obvious dichotomy. I am aware there are evil people in this world. In fact, they intrigue me. I find myself wanting to study people's behaviors. I am sure this intrigue comes from the depths of my morass and despair, from those times, I found myself at the bottom of a hollow place in life, scratching and clawing to get out yet stuck. In these times, the accurate assessment of how I wound up there would slowly and ever so clearly emerge.

I am not sure when I realized sinning makes us sick inside. Think about it. Think about a time you did something you knew to be wrong. A lie. A cheat. Greed or even sinful sexual desire. Then fast forward yourself to the place your mind wound up right after the dirty deed had passed. Yes, the place we go to when internally we grab for the drink or drug of choice, the distraction, or the sleep.

The ever so clever ability to tell ourselves we are not bad people, to justify the sin, or the breadth of it is meaningful. We experience an attraction to actions that feed a skin or flesh addiction, to pulse racing feelings of excitement, or the allure of the forbidden fruit.

I was infinitely attracted to the flame of sin in my lifetime. I loved its flickering heat; I yearned for it for many years, even decades. I was not some out-and-proud sinner who waved my sinful flag on the front porch of my home for the world to see. I did not walk around with a scarlet letter on my jacket to announce me when I entered a room. I was, like most humans, able to kick dirt on top of my crap and walk away, telling myself lies so I could live with myself. I ran with people my whole life who lived the entire range of being the best people in the world and the worst people in the world. I know this is a wide range. I loved the people who surrounded me in the depths of my sins and goodness. I was constantly pulled back to goodness, even when I did not want to be. And yet I would continue choosing to live in my sinful ways, even when I had to medicate and mask those decisions.

In truth, I had fun when I was sinning and took guilty pleasure in it. I loved my unhealthy habits and my vices. I could sit in the trenches of the world on my Harley Davidson and not be off-put by the dredges of society. I have been gifted with the eyesight to find greatness in all people.

For many years, I lived and thrived and shrunk and died, driven by my sins. I saw the same behaviors in other people. I saw men and women whose sinning behavior I disliked, and I would not say anything; I chose to live with the knowledge of their infidelity.

For me, when I veered from the path God called me to follow, everything fell apart. Everything. My vices started making me sick, my family slowly fell apart, and I started questioning my self-respect and worth. I realized I could no longer do what I used to and get away with it.

In fact, I came to really scary realizations about sinners. I am not afraid to say I have watched friends die from their sins and vices. Many. I watched a friend tell a lie about something and then get on his motorcycle and wrap himself around a tree. I watched a man attempting to cheat on his wife and a few weeks later he died while playing basketball. I watched a greedy man I worked with drop dead of a heart attack, a gluttonous woman die in her hotel room during a conference while eating herself into an insulin attack, and more.

Sinning will kill you; make no mistake. One way or another, even if it is a slow death brought on by silencing the mind. We are NOT wired to stay sinners even though we are born hardwired to be drawn to sin.

There is a deep chemical imbalance with it all. And those who figure it out correct course, save themselves, and live an unusually long and vibrant life. I swear to God I am a believer one hundred percent.

We are born into this world the most innocent of people as the purest versions of ourselves and, slowly but surely, we migrate towards sin. In our lives, if we are lucky, religious-based practices are introduced to us, and we find the ability to call upon the welcoming and mysterious power we sense lurking around us. For many of us, myself included, our belief system from the Bible anchors us and spells out the sins of past leaders to guide us.

I believe far too many of us are deaf to our moral barometers and have been over-written by our physical attractions, demons, and devices that lure us and create impossible temptations.

I wish I could say writing all of this is easy, but it is not. I feel a bit hypocritical in advising we listen to our beliefs, as I did not adhere to my internal wiring. Too often, across many parts and years of life, I ignored my right from wrong voice, the intuition I knew to be correct. I chose to give in to the intoxicating physical attraction to sinful practices. I admit this.

When you read this and wonder, I am born again in this way. Only in recent years have I fully committed myself to a complete life of honesty and integrity. In doing this, I have become stronger with greater confidence than ever, a better person, confidant, human, and teacher. Everything changes when you make this commitment.

What defeats our good internal mojo is our outward inability to adhere to a set of moral ethics. We drown feelings of shame in waves of false pleasure, an ebb and flow that robs us of our self-worth. It is a steep price tag, and when compounded, costs about everything.

If I could ask you twenty questions at this point about your life and nobody but you could answer them, how would you answer? Will you give yourself permission to be brutally honest? Will you listen to the truths you knew at birth before life's temptations overwrote your moral code?

Only you will know your answers to these questions. Be honest with yourself. This is not a test with right or wrong answers. It is a litmus revealing your truth, only to you, in this moment.

Give yourself one point for each YES answer. There is a key at the end of this exercise.

1. Do you ever lie? (Including little lies, sometimes.) Yes, or No?

2. Do you ever steal? (No matter how small.)

3. Do you ever fib when telling stories? (Even if you steer from exact truths in your story telling.)

4. Do you ever say something you do not mean? (For example, I will do this when you know you will not, or I will not do this when you know you will?)

5. Do you ever wish ill on other people in your head? (Be honest.)

6. Do you ever tell yourself the lie you are telling is going to help or be for a worthy cause? (This is the lie we tell ourselves about lying, ironically.)

7. Do you ever pretend you are something you are not?

8. Do you ever answer questions about yourself with a lie as the answer? (How old are you? Insert lie about age. If so, answer is yes.)

9. Would you ever cheat on your partner, spouse, or lover? Do not say NO, if you know the answer is yes; again this is a self-test, and requires brutal honesty.

10. Are you currently breaking your marriage or relationship vows?

11. Are you living any lies? (For instance, if you told someone you once went to Europe, but you never did, for example?)

12. I have lied about how much money I have.

13. I have lied about my weight.

14. I have lied about how much I exercise.

15. I have lied about where I live.

16. I have lied about where I work.

17. I have lied about my education.

18. I have lied to myself many times.

19. I know I am being lied to, but I will not confront it because if I do, I might lose the person I am in a relationship with.

20. I hang around people who I know lie.


KEY: Add the number of yes answers you gave.
1. 0          I am a saint! (Or, close to it.)
2. 1-5        Mere Lies!
3. 6-10       Moderate Liar!
4. 11-15      Liar, Liar!
5. 16-20      Pathological Liar!

Based upon where your total yes answers fall in these four categories, you have diagnosed yourself as someone who is living in a daily perpetual state of atmospheric bullshit or someone who avoids willful sin and lying.

How hard is it to correct course? The answer varies based on where your truth falls within the depth of the above scale. I would ascertain it is terribly difficult for the person who is an eleven or higher to change course without drastic lifestyle alteration. I believe most people in that range would not be shaken out of sinning by anything less than tragic or traumatic events occurring in their life to set them entirely on a new course.

The most important question for you to consider is about YOUR Journey to the Truth. Do YOU want to be more honest?

Yes, or No?

I hope yes. If so, read on, please. We will spend the rest of this book unpacking the methodology of how you can course correct in a way that gives you complete and utter control of your life like never before, and with it, tremendous food for the soul and success.

*CHAPTER 6*

# Living in Ruins

One day you wake up and look around and can hardly recognize your life. Have you had this experience? When I look back, I clearly see times where I ruined everything. This is the first time I have ever publicly said it like this, but it is completely true. I have ruined my life as I knew it several times over selfish desire for attention and lust or love.

It may be hard for people to reason with this knowing me today. I think most who know me today would never expect me to be someone who would carelessly ruin my life or others in the wake of seeking desires of the flesh. I look back in hindsight, and I cringe at my actions.

This realization alone made me think about the times people warned me of my unruly behavior or told me I was heading in the wrong direction. I could spend the rest of my life trying to make up for what I have done and never come close to fixing the hurt and damage created. Even worse, while this was happening, I blamed other people and things, reasons, and excuses for the results of my making semi-conscious fatal decisions about my relationships. I own it.

The truth is I had an insatiable appetite for attention at some point in my life. An unfillable void temporarily topped off by whatever current form of attention I craved. Most often, it was fulfillment of male attraction. I am a lover inside and out. I have loved love in my lifetime. I have loved to be loved. I foolishly put the weight of it above all things. It has given me such poor ROI.

When I had real love and true love, I pilfered it away, and I expended it for an addiction to attention. I hurt incredible people in the process, and I can never take it back. They know who they are. They have lived a life watching my self-sabotage, and I am not sure any of them have stayed around in the margins of my life long enough to see what I turned it into.

In truth, I could also say every man I ever was with cheated on me, and the statement would be true. But to say they did it before I ran away into the arms of someone else, I honestly do not know. I think many of them got away with their actions, ultimately unprovable. Still, with all the signs, I reacted to those beliefs of infidelity by countering them with an I will match you and raise you one scenario. The difference was, and still is, in looking back, their affairs were fleeting nights of one-off, whereas I went all in with my whole deck in a new direction, with a new man, and left them in my wake with a sudden preemptive departure. This was my ego telling me I deserved better while doing worse. There was no honor in how I acted. There was no truth in my unforgiving revenge.

I have cast many people to survivor island, for lack of better terms, where I would never visit again. For most of my life, my attitude backed by action was one of if you hurt me, you were done in my book. I closed the door in your face. I locked it and threw away the key. I was relentless in how I responded to people who did not hold me in what I considered to be the highest regard.

I know this sounds unsavory. Yet outside of the relationship zone during those parts of my life, I was quite successful. I was leading companies, ranking amongst the top salespeople in my firms. I was growing my business and wealth. My life was financially on track to an extremely high regard. I was caring for my family and my friends, and I was leading a fun and exciting life. By outward measures, my life was charmed.

And yet, if you were within my inner circle, there is no doubt you knew how broken I was. You knew my addictions and my vices. You knew of my self-sabotage and ruin. There were many cohorts during these troubled times in my life who were happy to join in the debauchery, and I cannot judge them as I did every inch of the sinning they did. They were, in many ways, some of the most beautiful, torn, and lost souls I have ever met. Many have died of the very same vices. Many of them are living empty lives still. I made it out, in the end, somehow, but they did not. I have buried many mates who lived that ragged and wretched life outside the lines and confines of the laws of good men. They died of their sins, gluttonies, and neglect, and many still are. I do not judge.

I have come to terms in my life with an understanding that God gave me these experiences so I would become less judgmental. I am, unlike self-loving aristocrats who think they are mightier than (and may be). I do not scoff at the likes of people like I ran with when I was young and free, stupid, and relentless in my pursuit for the edge of the cliff.

It is even hard to recognize myself sometimes when I look back compared to who I am today. It's hard to face the way I was, remember what I did, and consider the waste of my life and money. The time I spent on sinful ways and things all while telling myself I was living my best life when, in fact, I was totally misaligned, wasting my life while risking my life.

That is the truth.

The gift finding this truth has brought. Now, when I pass the beggar or the blighted, I see their soul peering through the dirt-covered face, and I know I could have slid down a few more notches to incredibly dark places not far from where I landed at some points in my life. Living as I did, poor, often addicted to vices, hurting inside, hurting outside, hurting others and myself, I now realize it has created a rich dictionary of experiences I draw on to help others climb out of their horrible places.

I now recognize, after fighting and battling my way through dark places, this undeniable set of horrible experiences has taught me an extremely valuable lesson about myself. I have seen the fragility of temptation and the inability to withstand vices. I have looked at myself in utter disgust, and I have lived with suffocating internal strife. I have learned my lessons the hard way, not by one mistake at a time but by repeating many mistakes many times. I believe the human will to right itself is stronger than the will to wrong ourselves.

While this battle may take many a good man down, it is a battle people everywhere are fighting. There are horror stories we know nothing about behind the crooked and forced smiles of our co-workers and the strangers we pass in the aisles at the grocery stores. We could never understand the depths of the heartache people live with daily, the loneliness, and the demons they are battling. Some families live in the wake of ruin, trapped by sickness and the incredible intoxication of lust because they cannot seem to get it right, find the path, let go of the vice, or correct course.

Many will lie and tell themselves they are too far down a path to turn around, as if walking deeper in the wrong direction is the only acceptable path. I tell you now, mindlessly going down the same path is not the only way.

Some will not save themselves. These do not deserve judgment; rather, I offer a tip of the hat, and acknowledgement because I know the enemy's strength. I know the battle. I know it is almighty and can take hold of you and not let go.

Today, I know how strong my will for survival is and how much I wanted to become the person others saw me as. And herein lies why I am dedicated to others today. I know my faith, hope, and belief in them can save them. The hope, faith, and belief in me given by others saved me. I know this to be true.

Today, I do not surround myself with perfect people. I look for people who want help. I look for people who need one other person to believe in them, who are willing to accept the belief, find hope and faith, and fight their way to honor. I am that one other person.

*CHAPTER 7*

# Bed Head

Perched atop a bunk bed, I can see the entire room. I am pushed into the corner, retreated from the world. I feel safe, protected, and secluded.

At home, growing up, privacy was a rarity, a privilege hardly ever experienced and yet greatly valued when found. I have memories of the bunk beds I laid in, maybe because I spent so much time contemplating my life lying in bed. I am pretty sure I solved my world problems from bed. My greatest ideas would be spawned there and spurred to epiphanies in the middle of the night, sending me straight out of bed to my journal, or later my iPhone notes, to capture a brilliant fleeting thought.

I loved the security and sanctity of being elevated and not easily reachable. My earliest memories of incredible thinking were when I was lying in my bed. I felt safe there, free to dream. Ironically, I remember retreating to the far corner from my father once when in dire trouble. I can't recall the exact grievance causing me to flee to my private heights, but I do remember my father's sweeping and angry arm reaching in to grab me and pull me down to face justice. Still, it was my place then, and I remember vividly something rare for me today as my memory is fading.

As I grew older, I shared a room with two twin-size beds. Mine was tucked against the wall opposing my sister's bed. I spent many nights here dreaming my first thoughts of boys. Love was on my mind for the first time. I was smitten with this curly-haired boy in the eighth grade. We shared my very first kiss, and I often dreamt of him while lying in bed.

I also lay there crying, sad, and longing for all of my wants and dreams, which were seemingly impossible. At that young age, everything seemed out of reach. I left behind the blissfully ignorant stage of childish innocence, coming to be aware of all we could not afford as a family, to knowing full well I could not afford much of what I desired, whether it be clothing, school trips, or projects. Many things were beyond my grasp. Such were my high school years.

When I finally left home and joined my then boyfriend in my first away-from-home living, I found myself lying in an old, full-size waterbed. I don't really recall how we filled it, but I believe we ran a hose through a window behind the headboard to the outside faucet attached to the side of the house.

The apartment was near the college I had chosen to seek a part-time secondary education (sponsored by scholarships).

Our bedroom was nestled deeply down a hall, through another room, and had sweeping swinging doors, like the old western saloon doors, except they went all the way to the floor and dragged against the shag carpet, making a swooshing sound when pushed or pulled.

This sound would later protect my boyfriend and me when a middle-of-the-night intruder came to call. After a night out drinking, he decided to visit a past resident of our apartment and rudely startled us awake, only to be met with a violent greeting by a swinging shower rod not yet installed from our recent move.

We would not stay in that first apartment long. The waterbed joined the rest of our meager belongings to be ensconced in a single-story home located in a nearby town.

During this part of my life, I was met with great turmoil. Now clearly seen in hindsight, my own bad decisions led me to a place in my life where I was honestly not mature enough to navigate.

The dark secrets of my world were too unruly to be brought to light to my normal confidants, like my dad or mom. Even my siblings couldn't be let inside the tiny house of horrors where I lived.

I had allowed evil to sneak in through my relationship, bringing the sheltered child I was an introduction to wrongdoings, addictive vices, and non-integral characters.

My first steps into the world away from home into a life I hoped would be youthful and playful became a routine of ill practices and zero adult guidance. I lay in that waterbed often and cried for my mom and dad, whom I knew I could not call to come save me because I had chosen to leave home against their wishes. Now I was stuck.

I have thought about this my whole life, too; how important it is to tell our burgeoning young adult children when they leave home, no matter the bind or predicament you find yourself in, I promise you can call. There will be no arguing or judgement, if you need to leave, find safety, or get help. I had only my mother's words haunting me, "You will be back." The last thing I wanted to do at my tender age, starting my adult life, was for her to be right and me to be wrong.

I stayed in that place, in that relationship, far longer than I should have. I stayed through years of denial and fear spiraling inevitably down to a climactic, traumatic night when a decision had to be made. Bed during those years became the only safe place I could hide when I wanted distance between my newly formed vices and the sins of my peers.

On one of the last and final nights of my stay in this dark part of my life, I was taken hostage in my room. True story. I will leave the details out as the people involved have turned their lives around and been long since forgiven by me.

Suffice it to say I endured a whole night of horror there. On this night God got my attention. I was given strength through a shocking and painful jolt of reality to know I had to leave. Awareness came to me in a shattering of the safe-haven I had always found in my bed. I, who is not and never will be a victim, was allowing myself to be victimized. I had to act.

I did leave in the middle of the next night with the assistance of a few close friends. Freeing and exiting myself from this life came with harshness the likes of which I prefer never to return to again.

The page turned, and a new bed emerged. I bought a plain box spring and mattress and found a suitable apartment, moving in with three girls who ranged from my age to half a dozen years older.

The new place was a house belonging to an old artist now retired and moved on; his family all grown. The four of us shared a sprawling estate, splitting the rent. My room was the artist's den, easily the size of three bedrooms.

Freedom is the word that comes to mind when I think of the huge empty room containing a small full-size box spring and mattress with no headboard and just little ol' me and a few boxes of my belongings. I desired to be free from the chains I had been bound by and found my way to a new life. A new environment bred the ability for me to renew my commitment to a healthier version of myself. I had a new circle of friends, a new outlook on life, and a new taste of adulthood in a brighter, more optimistic way.

My choice to stay in this town, one town over from where I had moved originally and still far from home, surprised many, including my now ex-boyfriend, who had moved on straight away with a local girl. He followed me for the longest time, watching my movement from job to home. I know he was hurt but his behavior became alarming but fortunately his life choices forced him to stop haunting me. It would be a long struggle before he found his way and his vices, which also plagued me, continued unabated for decades.

In hindsight, my intuition to flee was one of great salvation. I clearly saved myself from a life wretched with sin and addictive vices. I was easily enticed by the dark side of the moon, having lived a very straight life before leaving home.

I was not adequately wired for living on the dark side. The guilt and shame I felt when doing wrong would kill me inside, and my barometer pushed me to the right side every time. See, I had a deeply embedded sense of right from wrong, and no matter how off the beaten path I went, there was always the pull back to alignment for me. I did not consciously recognize this. I was fighting an internal subconscious GPS system. Had I consciously recognized this during this time in my life, I could have avoided a lot of future harm.

My life took me next on a new path with a new person. Over the next decade, I spent time with this beautiful person and shared a few homes with him. My full-size freedom bed carried me through to bigger and better furniture and times.

When the romance and flames of this decade waned, I was once again alone and renting a nearby apartment. I lay in bed weeping at night from the hurt and harm of lost love and direction. All over again. In this same bed, I lay awake pondering self-recognized brokenness.

It wasn't always about men, however. As I searched for understanding regarding my relationship with my mother, a counselor prescribed a book, *My Mother, Myself* which changed my life. I lay in bed reading, learning, understanding plaguing emotions and stresses I had contemplated for many years.

Over the next two decades, different beds became my solace. In a grand poster bed, I contemplated my new name, enjoyed the shine of a newlywed, experienced the joys of ten long months of pregnancy, and awoke in hard labor anticipating the birth of my son.

Later, I lay alone, crushed by a relationship lost and broken for years. Those nights were long and painful. I endured many sleepless nights and once again found myself fighting angst.

In bed is where I thought of my company name, where I thought of my next move in life, where I solved my own problems and those of my clients and friends.

Bed Head is the title of this chapter because I believe this is where we are close to our souls, our hearts and mind, and our spiritual vision. The release of the day found in our beds is where our souls take flight, where we heal our brokenness, and where we retreat to safety. To this day if I am sad, hurting, or sick, I retreat to my bed to rest, to contemplate, and to escape.

Bed. The place where the vision of my most significant accomplishments were born. I realized on this journey to the truth and finding honor, there is irony. I always felt my physical attractions drove me away from my best version of myself. The oxymoron of bedding down as applied to sin and lust or integrity and salvation is thick in contrast and complexity. I think it shows how close we all are to correcting our paths, mere inches apart. The two lives lay, unbeknownst to us, one side a dark path, the other a bright light. A simple turn to the right or left gives us an entirely different perspective, an entirely different outlook and path.

How strong is the voice driving us? I think the answer lies in our physical make up and life's timing. We are more apt to be strong against the wiles of sin when we are strong in character and the wisdom of past scars and mistakes. We are far less likely to choose the long-and-hard road, and our decision-making becomes wiser and more logical than the whims and woes of our youthful dreams and desires. The consequence is unavoidable to think about at some intersection in life. We can no longer be blissfully ignorant of the cost or price of such things.

As an addendum to Bed Head, I am apt to say out loud bed is where I will die. No doubt. I hope to die having laid everything I have for life lessons and work on the table for future generations to read and contemplate.

As I write these words from 35K feet in the air, on my way home from vacation with Cory and Jagger, I think about how magical it would be when I am long gone for people to read these words, these lessons. Parents can pass them along to their children, and college students and groups might stumble upon the many psychological readings and study the human aspects of its truth and application. I hope so.

Or you will be reading this from your bed and you in fact will get Bed Head too! Touché.

In closing this chapter, I pay homage to some incredible blankets. I laugh out loud writing this. I could write a book on the beds and blankets of my life and maybe one day I will. There have been many incredible ones.

My favorite right now is a winter white Afghan I won in NJ at a Brownstone hosting a friend's charity event. An elder sewed it and donated it for raffling. It is soft and worn, beautiful and warm. It was created by a soul who loved it and gave it away in love, won with the pledge of donated monies, and loved by the winner. Yes. Homage to the blankets.

# CHAPTER 8

# Reflected Hate

A quote from Marian Keyes has always stuck with me: "The things we dislike most in others are the characteristics we like least in ourselves." Likewise, Carl Jung said, "Everything that irritates us about others can lead us to an understanding of ourselves."

One day it hit me like a ton of bricks. I was a hypocrite. I caught myself, like so many of us will who have a fair share of self-reflection, loudly putting someone down for gossiping, something I had regularly been doing the same way.

I felt guilty over a conversation in which I had participated in and quite frankly was in poor character. I would argue the propensity to gossip is a taught trait, and in my case, likely stemming from a loud example I had seen my whole life. In truth, those I had talked about were good people who had bad luck or made bad choices. Gossiping about them stood only to deplete my internal worth.

Let me repeat the last part of the paragraph more loudly for everyone in the back:

Engaging in gossip shows bad character ONLY STANDS TO DEPLETE OUR OWN SELF-WORTH.

No one can become stronger or better by crapping on other people. I recall seeing a meme reading, "Your candle will not shine brighter by blowing someone else's out." Wow! What a true statement.

Why do we gossip? As is alluded to in this chapter's title, Reflected Hate, when we vocalize against others it reflects what we internally dislike in ourselves. Why do we do this? My study has led me to conclude, psychologically speaking, we are denouncing this character trait by speaking, as if by saying it we will change. The louder we get, the closer we are to solving the riddle of our own moral gaps.

It is as if on some level we know we are veering off the path and our internal wiring is willing us back on course. We find ourselves talking to others about what we hope to change in ourselves.

Did you know this? Is this concept a revelation for you? Is it ringing true for you? Let this lead to reflection of what we hate in ourselves. Have you been listening to your own gossip?

On January 1st, 2018, I made a promise to no longer gossip. Coaching with Jay guided me to understand this concept. It was a life-changing decision. The moment I realized this; I was forever changed. I knew what I had taken out was not going back in the jar. Ignorance became awareness, leaving me with the choice to act towards improvement. I had to either reject what I now knew to be truth and honor and continue down the same path or turn away and take action towards improvement.

At the time, I was unaware of how this would impact and change my internal confidence and self-love. I only knew I did not like how I felt when I was not acting in good character.

When I committed to no gossip, I immediately became aware of how much I gossiped. At every turn throughout the initial days, while conversing with family, on phone calls, and in social circles, I caught myself about to speak words whose sole purpose was to spread gossip. I suddenly began experiencing a haunting feeling, and thoughts of past conversations entered my mind. It was as if I walked out of a fog, step by step, into the sun.

I found myself incredibly embarrassed while at the same time, understanding why I received the reactions I had in gossip-filled conversations. In fact, like spinning a Rolodex of good to bad character, I could see in my friends' personalities those who participated deeply in this behavior and those who would listen and choose not to participate, ending the conversation quickly.

I felt embarrassed for not knowing how off-putting my commentary had been. I also realized this was an unconscious, lingering lesson taught early in my childhood. In fact, it was a problem within my own family. I believe it to be behavior borne from ignorance which speaks to a lack of education rather than any lack of character. There are generations of unaware and untaught humans making small talk and neighborly chatter, unaware of its sinful nature, unaware of its harmful nature, and its useless purpose. We waste time, create hurt, deter our relationships, and impede progress when we engage in self-worth depleting gossip. Whether we draw on the religious connotation of it being one of the Ten Commandments or if we simply listen closely to what it does to our psyche, we know it leaves us feeling inadequate and pulls us away from our internal trust system.

Let us expand on the trust system depletion factor as it is one of the greatest areas we can undertake for self-improvement, along with self-confidence, self-love, and self-worth. If we can make this difficult but eventually simple transition, the impact is wonderful.

Trust begins with our character, and we often relegate it to how others interact with us. The hurt and broken personality says, "I will trust you when you prove you can be trusted," as if trust is earned instead of immediately given and possibly depreciated through breaks in character.

Trust is how all connections should start. I build my initial relationship on trust, forgetting the past, the breaks, and hurts from others; I start with trust. Then, only when an individual shows their character is not built on honesty, do I lose trust.

Easily said, and yet difficult to apply.

But what if we are liars? What if we talk about others, gossip, and ridicule people for various reasons? Would you trust others if YOU are untrustworthy? Would you believe your coworkers were not discussing you behind their backs if in fact you constantly talked about others when someone left the room? The answer is no. You will not trust others if your character is lacking.

Conversely, your trust in others will be supreme when your character is strong. Again, "We hate in others what we hate in ourselves." How about, "We expect in others what we lack in ourselves." Or, "We distrust in others what we cannot be trusted to in ourselves." Do you see the pattern?

This changes everything, does it not? In our reflection and self-awareness, we can know this incredible and profound power:

WE CONTROL OUR OWN TRUST, LOVE, CONFIDENCE AND SELF-WORTH.

How we act, carry ourselves, and interact in our private spaces when no one is really keeping count is how we interact and find others of good character. Like attracts like.

What is the first step towards changing our reflected hate? Awareness is step one. Are you aware of your worst traits depleting you of self-love, worth, trust, and value?

Are you currently lying about something? Are you currently cheating on something or someone? Are you currently talking in disdain against others? Only you know the answers.

What if you changed and aligned yourself with the character you know internally is calling you to be good? What if you rid yourself, as difficult as it may be, of activities or actions, words, or thoughts which are character depleting? What then would be your reflection?

I am sure here is where I should add another ten steps. The truth is, I do not know what those steps are yet, and I am not through all the steps myself. When I took step one in Jan 2018, with self-awareness, it was horribly shocking to realize how riddled I was with bad actions.

Over time as I rid myself of these behaviors an unexpected consequence revealed itself. Eventually, I saw friends not on the same path wean themselves away from me. I believe they were subconsciously aware of my new direction. I am sure they found others available for conversations of hate and dismay towards others. I could not wait for them. My path led to a more incredible me. I felt rising self-confidence and a genuine love towards myself for the character I was vehemently displaying.

I did not realize how, in gaining new strength, I would begin to see character flaws in others. I found myself advising family members, pointing out the need for change as if a rehabilitated person sharing the beauty of the other side might. As might be expected, my words fell on deaf ears.

People will change when they are personally ready to or when they see fault or find a need to change, and not because the guy or gal standing next to them shares a life-altering epiphany. This is a sad truth in life.

Show me a couple who are both alcoholics and I will show you one partner who rehabilitates and leaves behind the other who cannot or is not ready to join.

I moved on, going beyond the place where I left behind friends who could not or would not follow. Realizing I was healing beyond my peers as I course-corrected, I found others whose character was like mine. This awareness was significant and led to the sad part of my story because I moved to a place where I simply no longer could, despite some folks' desire, continue the relationships.

I could no longer maintain these friendships. My mind, body, and soul would not allow me to give time to those friendships. Thus, I physically and mentally moved beyond.

Of course, those friends may still call and I speak should I encounter them, but I could not sit in those friendships as I once had. I simply had to gracefully exit stage left to the new world I lived in, passing in kind gesture, and still doing no harm but not lingering in a place I no longer wished to be. The evolution of my character willed me to a greater level of friendship.

# CHAPTER 9

# Unlearning: A Rebirth

At some point in my life, I realized a need to change behaviors and thoughts learned as a child. In truth, I am still unlearning when I recognize bad traits.

My need to change thoughts and behaviors is not to slight my childhood mentors, parents, or teachers. Learning I needed to unlearn led to a complete self-awareness I didn't even know existed until I was 40-plus years old.

Unlearning is a level of self-awareness I think some people never reach. We hate in others what we dislike in ourselves. I am grateful to God I found this place called unlearning and I hope reading this chapter helps many of you.

I will share some of what I have chosen to unlearn. This is not a complete list but it's thorough and hits the highest and worse traits to fix. I've learned not to:

- Interrupt others when they speak.
- Let my mind wander or consider my answer before someone finishes talking. I first listen to an entire statement before speaking.
- Lie. I had to learn not to lie or embellish for attention or effect.
- Chase physical attraction.
- Lose my focus.
- Dramatize.
- Display exceptional anger.
- Play it safe.

These innate habits truly deterred my relationships, personal growth, and overall self-love and happiness. I will break down each of these, describe in detail what they did to hurt me, and how I went about changing each.

## LISTENING AND HEARING WITH HONOR

I am not sure where I was when someone pointed out how badly I interrupted people, and I still catch myself doing it. I hate to admit it was a learned behavior, as I never want to make my upbringing sound a certain way, However, with the intent of making this lighter than it could be and living with three other women in my home growing up, getting a word in edgewise was a trick. I equate it to sitting on the side of a racetrack with a race car idling and trying to find the spot to jump back on the track. It requires careful grappling of the wheel, the force of a foot on the gas pedal, timing, and possibly a bit of eye closing and wishing too.

As a child, I interrupted almost every conversation I had. It was my normal method to enter into a discussion.

What came after busting into a conversation was even more interesting. I felt the need to say everything on my mind all jumbled together with no synchronicity to the message other than a desperate need to get it all out, right then, or lose my place in the invisible speaking line. I was the evidence, and the proof of a home environment which included a lot of talking.

Incredibly neither my parents or any others corrected me, and I carried this horrible, embarrassing habit into my business world where someone had the strength and fortitude one day to confront me about it. I remember it stinging to hear as I already knew it to be true. In the moment of realization, I heightened my self-awareness to it and slowly and methodically broke myself of the habit.

Breaking my habit of interrupting others was more difficult than I imagined, yet less tactical than I am explaining. I believed what I had to say was more important than what someone else was saying; thus, driving my need to speak.

I know how I felt when I was younger, as if the intelligent thing I was about to announce was going to magically set off bells and whistles as if God himself had spoken. I remember beaming with pride when sharing my idea; doing so exposed my deep and intricate mind with every word I said.

It's ironic how long it took, most of my life, to realize the parallel between saying something intelligent and how the challenge in its delivery affects the interpretation.

When I finally realized everything I had to say was not more important than the next person speaking, when I had a sense of calm about me in time and patience, I recognized it is a sign of respect to wait my turn, I learned a cadence of conversation I am certain is more enjoyable for those who talk to me today.

This is a constant work in progress for me. It is easy to divert back out of habit of course.

## LIES: THE WALK TO TRUE HONESTY!

Do you think you are honest? If you had asked me this question most of my life my answer would have been yes. Except for a few genuinely dark years where I knew I was not operating from an honest place and my pain was too profound to deny, I believe I have always been good and fair, kind and caring.

I know I colored outside the lines of true, actual total honesty. This might have been embellishing a story unknowingly or omitting parts making me look less than perfect. Never mind the deep end of this pool, intentional lies which steal happiness and peace.

Lying is both an art and a science. Can you identify a liar? Are YOU a liar? Answer this with the following key if you dare!

1 – 10 Scale. Consider 1 is being honest as Job and 10 is being a liar of deceitful magnitudes.

Where do you fall in this self-assessment?

If your answer is anything other than one or two then you have much work to do in what could be the most stubborn part of your walk. I assure you, it's worth the effort to do the self-work here to gain more out of your life, feel happier, and be more confident.

Take this walk towards honesty with me. And if you can't right now, there's no judgement being made. This chapter will be here in this book on your shelf to be picked up again any day and revisited.

Would you, for a moment, think about the last time you intentionally lied?

- Was it for a good and purposeful reason?
- Were you protecting someone or yourself?
- Were you avoiding conflict you didn't want to face?
- Was the lie for deceitful and self-serving purposes?
- More importantly, how did the lie make you feel inside?

Sit with your answer to this last question. Listen for and examine the internal conscious voice sending mental signals, and even physical ones, to say you are doing something sinful or wrong when you lie. Our conscience is the voice we ignore. It is this voice we strive to silence. Many people will drown this voice in alcohol or drugs, many will ignore its banging and clanging inside our souls, choosing to self-medicate away the internal feeling of angst against ourselves.

Ironically and hypocritically, the liars of the world are the same people who hold others to higher standards than they do themselves because nobody has ever taken the time to explain the internal toll lying takes on their physical, mental, and spiritual well-being. These same people, me included for many years, walk around judging others, and rise against an injustice they recognize easily in their interactions with others.

I am here today to tell you this behavior comes with a toll to pay. Not because I heard about it from someone else and not because I have seen it in the lives of many others. Rather, I have watched people tear their families apart for sinful reasons and because I, too, lived as a liar and destroyed happiness and love in my life. I was a hostage of my addiction to excitement and sought attention. I realized this about myself after years of careful counseling. There was a deficit, a hole. I was trying to fill a void I felt in maternal love and acceptance.

We sometimes enter the world as adults cracked and broken, and we don't even know it. When we measure our lives, all may look good on the surface, but just below lurks this illness we carry from emotions felt as a child, which have too long gone unfixed or recognized.

If nobody shows up to say you are broke when they see it, this road can be long and riddled with a lot of heartache and loss, as was the case for me. My most significant losses came from my own hand due to my lack of self-awareness from youth into adulthood. It would not change until I had suffered heartache and loss in my life and realized who I was and what I was.

My demise brought me to the point of threatening my life through self-sabotage and disdain. When I finally fell to the ground in the rubble of broken relationships and self-induced drug addictions indulged in numbing the screams of inner voices begging for correction, I looked into the mirror and asked God why.

I really didn't understand the role I played in my demise, until I repeated this several times. I hurt more than myself and I hurt others. I ruined incredible relationships and almost destroyed myself while not looking inward and denying ownership of what I had done to myself.

We can always point to and find excuses when we look for reasons to, when we look to find fault in others or in circumstances. Scattered through the streets are easy to find excuses, and we are wired to be attracted to excuses, as those allow us to avoid the pain of self-reflection, embarrassment, and real ownership. Avoidance doesn't allow us to heal or grow, just the opposite. Eventually, avoiding internal wrongdoing will bubble back up like a slow boiling pot until emotion overflows like an unattended pot in uncontrollable and unexpected ways.

I now know the unaddressed guilt and shame I carried wreaked havoc on my relationships because I was always walking wounded. Albeit invisible, my wounds shone brightly when any slight or perceived slight occurred against me. I was oversensitive and overreacted to hurtful things, and nobody understood why. The real damage happens when people don't feel supported.

Undertaking change at this level is a journey into the unknown, which is why few people ever truly heal. You can't fix what you won't admit is broken and you can't heal if you don't put in the work.

Ask yourself a couple of simple questions:

- Am I emotionally balanced?
- Do I respond to hurt, pain, and conflict in a healthy manner?

To expand, I am not asking you if you become angry when anger is called upon or sad when you're hurt. I am asking, is your reaction the correct LEVEL of response to the crime?

When you respond disproportionately with an 8, 9, or 10 anger level to what should be a 3, 4, or 5, reaction, it is inappropriate to the situation, perpetrator, and relationship, you are viewed as being emotional, illogical, and out of control. Most people faced with this level of uncalled-for anger will consider you dangerous. It will cause people to steer away from you and to feel unsettled at best and fearful at worst when around you. If it happens at work, it usually has consequences, keep you from advancing in leadership roles, and leaves you disconnected from peers, colleagues, managers, and subordinates. It puts you on an emotional island you are sure to feel.

Walking around the world with your invisible hurt and continuing to compound your emotional baggage will eventually weigh you down or break you. The weight of carrying this emotional baggage and stacking on more weight will break your back and toss you down an emotional hole. It may manifest as depression, anger management issues, broken relationships, or worse, lost relationships and at its worst have criminal consequences and do actual harm to yourself or others.

How far are you willing to go with your hurt unaddressed? Are you ready to chance your future and the future of your familial and friendly relationships on an ability to keep the jack in the box?

How much energy will you expel in trying to keep this under wraps and how long can it go like this before you have something dire occur in your life which makes you unavoidably brought to face it.

As you read this chapter, are you close to a breaking point as you read this chapter? If so, stop immediately and find someone professional or even personal but trustworthy to sit and talk with about your pain, your past, and your trauma. Seek personal care. You will not regret it. Over time you will realize the high-value ROI from facing these demons and working your way to health.

**CHASING PHYSICAL ATTRACTION:**

Let's admit it. We are animals. At the core of our existence, we are intellectual animals. We have wiring both physical and mental, and we have access to other realms of existence, both spiritual and faithful. We are complex beings with a GPS on autopilot which, without direction, will lead us to unconscious acts and leave us shameful and guilt-ridden. Some people define this as sin; others frankly don't label it and live with it.

Let me be clear. Throughout my life I have tried to be a good person. I have lived by a code of ethics I would put up against the average human and come out looking good (I think). In my lifetime as a young adult, I was drawn physically to the opposite sex. Naturally, as a young and energetic person, my physicality drew me to the lion. I had to steer those feelings and I am proud to say I didn't fully succumb to often-repeating physical attractions which occurred daily but had no direction other than an antenna towards sexual desire brought on by subconscious thinking.

I am not without sin. I have made poor decisions. However, I created clear boundaries for myself keeping me out of the deep ditches of sin. I never went home from a bar with a man I had just met, ever, which begs for anyone to come forth saying otherwise. It simply never happened. I could not bring myself even when I was physically attracted and even when I was impaired by alcohol, to bed down with a man with whom I didn't have an existing long-term and likely relational future with.

In reflection, this realization was everything for self-love for me, and I am not saying I judge those around me who chose otherwise. I have had a front-row seat often to this behavior choice in others. I didn't understand my friends who chose to do such a thing, but I also didn't look at them in disdain. I accepted the ideology of sex as more personal and intimate than a physical act to me. I denied myself relief from the unquenchable thirst at times because I morally would not give myself to anyone I didn't love or whom I did not think had the intention and potential to be my mate in life. As a result of this thinking and this living, I was a good partner to my mates.

In truth, I did allow myself physical interaction when I was single with male friends whom I trusted and whom I dated on a longer-term basis, but to put my dance card up against someone my age, I think my numbers look prudish.

I share this whole thought process about self-control because a desire to help women decide their boundaries is one of my deepest secrets. I will tell you I have a lot of self-respect because of this. My whole life many assumed me to be the person who bedded people I worked with. It simply isn't so. There were instances when I was attracted to men I worked with, but I always kept myself in control; I wanted the respect of my male counterpart in the board-room.

Was this a strategy? Yes. I saw what happened to women who didn't hold themselves in this regard in the office. My female counterparts who gave themselves freely and sexually found themselves not taken seriously and often relegated to lesser stature in the pools of leadership and management.

I believe this choice was made, not because of a lack of experience or merit, but out of lack of integrity. Yes, the double standard is real. What's good for the gander is not always good for the goose. Knowing the double standard existed meant knowing you needed to abide by this unpopular and unwritten rule or face consequences and career demise if you failed to navigate the perilous flight chosen.

Intellectually we fight the notion and deny the double-standard matters. I saw it play out too many times with ruin for the woman to deny its reality. Once a woman lost the battle to resist the physical attraction, her losses mounted and, for most, were catastrophic.

I am fortunate to have avoided this plight. I had to unlearn the natural physical autopilot driven by my loin and learn to use my brain to guide me. It is a battle lost by many humans.

Are you in control of your physical flight? Do you believe there is a price tag of self-worth or integrity if you do or don't follow this internal wiring of your mind and soul over your physical desires? I wonder if you have ever given it true thought. I wonder, too, if you're a man reading this if the answers stack up differently than those provided by females. I bet it does. Maybe not. It's not for me to say. You know the truth now. Give this honest thought as change is a worthy choice in this battle. Consider your boundaries in your mind. Control what you have always thought was uncontrollable. Find the strength which flows from desiring change. You will thank yourself one day.

## LOSING MY FOCUS

How many times in your life have you driven down an intentional road only to see a butterfly, take a sudden turn, and find yourself down an unknown road with no idea how to get back?

Are you someone who struggles with attention deficit disorder? I am. I was diagnosed with it long ago. Interestingly my output is rock star level. I execute on a high, high level but it's a learned skill. To become someone who crosses my ts, on schedule, on time, and has tremendous power and output, I had to learn organizational traits, priority management, time management, and self-control. In addition, here's the big one: I had to learn to accept I am easily distracted, recognize when it happens, and lock myself back into the task by back tracking several steps and re-starting from where I left off hundreds of times a day.

Let this sink in. Are you able to do this? Can you keep the strings of your day sewn together and stay on a path to an end, fruition, and execution? It is a practiced skill, and it can be done. There is no cure...but I am a high-functioning person with ADD who creates high output. ADD is not an excuse to use for poor execution. I am living proof. One day, I will write a book about this.

Did you know people diagnosed with ADD and even ADHD (Attention Deficit Hyperactivity Disorder) are often highly intelligent, fast-paced, and genius thinkers? It's true. By labeling ADD and ADHD as mental illnesses, the stigma attached implies the person is slow or a slow learner or thinker. In reality, the opposite is true. Do ADD/ADHD humans struggle to sit still in a classroom environment? Yes. Is the teacher failing to keep up with the student's fast thinking and learning capabilities? Are others missing the high stimuli needed to keep a high thinker moving in thought? Yes, to both questions.

Who pays the price? Who is required to adhere to the classroom setting? Doctors prescribe medications to children with ADD/ADHD to slow them down, to 'help' them fit the group mold and sit still. We force them to act unnatural for their personality, to slow down, be still, and call it a victory.

Whose victory is it? There is less classroom disruption, it's less annoying for the teacher and less interruptive for others. Whom are the ones hurt in this scenario? The student, the child, and the person labeled with a stigma and who is given less and made to feel they are weird or not normal.

For the past several hundred years, we revered and celebrated those geniuses who created the world we now live in, who invented the unthinkable, and who drove entrepreneurship and risk taking to new heights out of genius-level thoughts only inspired by a natural setting in which the thinker could perpetrate the creative mind to paper and then drive it into existence. Do you think in a hundred years we will be better by extinguishing the light of today's potential genius? I am guessing not.

To my fellow ADD and ADHD-labeled humans, take your meds, especially if they help you slow an out-of-control mind. Find a balance applying self-discipline without dulling your senses to unlock the gift of brilliance you were given. Teachers, please tell your students who fit into this category how extraordinary their minds are and work to help them manifest future inventions, genius philosophies, and creations. Our future, the future of our children, and our legacy depends on us getting this right.

I had to unlearn having ants in my pants. I had to learn to control my thoughts. I had to learn to live with my brilliance, harness it, and allow it to guide me to genius thinking and ideas without derailing my everyday productivity. I have learned to use a technique called the Work Burst. The Work Burst method concentrates on hours of focused work having the equivalent of many long hours. It is my superpower and the superpower of many I teach and train to harness their power. I built three companies and my career, meandering crookedly along a path by way of short bursts of concentrated and powerful work.

## DRAMATIZING

Who me? Nah. [Laugh out loud.]

I was born in the woods under a tree by a pack of drama wolves. Sounds right to me. In all seriousness, I would put my family against any other family who thinks it has cornered the market on drama and then double down my bet, knowing we would win.

Born from drama, amongst drama, and around drama, I am, of course, dramatic. I have a flair for deep adjectives in my vocabulary when describing things. I am an excellent storyteller, not missing any insatiable detail for the onlooker listening to the gritty details of emotion, woe, or whimsical happenings. You will want to sit at our family table when at a party as we will be the ones laughing the loudest.

Conversely, we are the ones crying the hardest. We are the ones living in an extraordinary level of pain, an unrelenting, seemingly perpetual unluckiness. Ask us any day and we will tell you, nobody has it harder than we do.

This is the mentality and habitual way of seeing the world I had to unlearn. I had to figure out my penchant for the negative aspects of looking at things and find my silver linings when wrongdoing did occur. I had to unlearn speaking out loud every time I experienced transgression in my life so as not to spill the sour soup onto others. I had to unlearn seeking sympathy as a means of comfort when I experienced the slightest hint of bad things. I had to unlearn bitching and moaning, seemingly a sport in my family of exaggerative magnitudes. I looked around one day and realized our deficits and misgivings were not any worse than those experienced by any other family. Everyone in the world has a fair share of bad things happening on a regular basis.

I set out to unlearn my reactions and learn not to spread drama. I learned coping mechanisms for when drama found me. I had to de-sensationalize my world, if such a word exists. I strive to adhere to living a de-sensationalized life.

Sadly, I am the only one in my family who has chosen to unlearn this mindset. I am surrounded by drama and often drown sitting in family discussions, verbally whipped by a thousand lashes of the tongue. I am aware and at times I physically leave the conversation when I cannot cope without a break. It is as if the very words would kill me if even one more was spoken. My disdain for negativity and negative drama can make me feel physically ill. I feel as if I escaped a prison when I learned to de-sensationalize.

I sometimes make fun of this reality, but the unlearning I did here is no minor undertaking. It taught me to use dramatic thinking to create beauty: beautiful writings, teachings, classrooms, and events. I have harnessed all of it to a positive place with great ROI, and it's a productive part of my life. I am a drama queen; A productive, caring, and kind drama queen.

## EXCEPTIONAL ANGER

What level of anger in a situation is acceptable? On a scale of 1-10 with ten being uber angry and scary, where do you fall when your top pops off? Does your top pop off?

I am a professional top popper. Without question I have a temper. I recall being seen by a doctor as a toddler for holding my breath until I passed out. Yes, you heard right. When I didn't get my way, I held my breath until I passed out. I did this several times, and the doctor told my mother to "walk away from her" and "don't give in," and so began my journey of having others leave me over my anger. Good advice, do you think? I am guessing it was proper medical advice. I can tell you for myself, I am still working on this.

I have never taken anger management classes, or been counseled for my anger, although I am certain I could use this training. However, I have spent a long time, decades, learning to harness my anger, and appreciating my angst as a superpower driving me to greater things.

Anger can be a fuel, and it doesn't always need to manifest in bad or negative situations. Take, for instance, someone who really pisses you off. What if you turned right around and went to work on something productive? Even if the work was motivated by your desire to shove it up their ass, do you agree it could be effective? The answer is YES!

Some form of anger fueled my whole life, and I have built success harnessing anger as a superpower. Feeling misunderstood is what I have been most angry about my entire life.

During my childhood I felt misunderstood. Inside I felt like I was someone different than who people saw or could see by means of my clothing or my economic stature. I felt like I was a winner, yet I knew others did not see the same 'me' I saw. I often walked around mad internally because I felt overlooked.

I found ways to draw people into my world so they could have a better look. I entered science fairs and dance competitions. I pushed myself to the top of the charts in any group setting, curriculum, or sport to test my mental and physical boundaries and show the world the greatness I saw.

As an adult, I understand my part in this, maybe I didn't fully believe in myself, and I did not have the tools to express my feelings except through anger.

Today, I believe I am great. By great I mean, someone who is good at a higher level than most people. I am someone who has high output and someone who does excellent things regularly. I am not afraid to say this out loud, and I no longer think it's bad for a person to have strong inner confidence.

When insecurity was driving and I tried to look great, my greatness was hidden by a cloak draped over someone quite broken. I spent a long time wearing the invisibility cloak. Today I am cloak-free, and I feel good about feeling great.

I still live with anger. I become furious at times. I still need to put myself in time-outs. I have spent a long time with Jay Doran talking about leaning into conflict. This effort has taught me to see my personal relationship with anger and harness it to the degree I am less likely to burn the house down metaphorically and more likely to walk away and go for a run. And when I can't walk away because sometimes my feet are just glued in place, I stand and speak my peace and live with the consequences, of which there are plenty. I can do this knowing I was honest and spoke the truth, angry or not.

I have discovered my anger is deeply rooted in integrity, and when I see what I perceive as duplicity, I am like a superhero striking out to battle evil. I am far more willing to fight than most of my peers. Wearing the anger suit is more comfortable today. I can live with who I am and how I am. Every day is a constant work in progress; an acknowledgment, and proof of how converting anger to production and providing control and direction for this double-edged superpower is invaluable.

The greatest thing to come from my life-taught anger management lessons is my ability to help others in this area. It's an epidemic of proportions in the world and using myself as an example helps me connect with people. It permits people who carry guilt and shame over anger to accept it is healthy to unload instead of carrying it. This understanding is freeing and liberating and calibrating all at once for them. It is a gift I am happy to hand out.

## PLAYING IT SAFE

Taking risks has never been my strong suit. I don't know if this is because I lived the first two decades of my life not having enough to squander. I don't even like leaving food on my plate. To say I have a conservative mindset is an understatement. I am practical, although a dreamer. I will examine things three times, then act. I will measure things out of a desire to be accurate and as if my life depended upon it to be accurate. For me, the saying measure twice cut once is more like measure ten times then think about cutting. Indeed, a painful reality for me.

How have I come so far down a risky road to success? How did I take the massive chance and risks needed to reach where I am now? It's like I climbed a tall mountain without a Sherpa, having no clue how scary reaching each peak would be until after looking back from the summit of each peak to appreciate the distance climbed and truly wincing at the thought of the risk I mindlessly pushed through.

Take building my current company. I left a high-paying job for non-paying self-employment in a saturated field with a high deficiency rate. How did I ever step out of the gates on day one? I can tell you: I was dying where I was. I don't even know how it happened, but I was starting to die in my old job, brought on by time and circumstance. Every day was torturous. I felt under appreciated and overlooked for my skill. To onlookers I appeared to be having one of those hold-your-breath temper tantrums. The more I think about it, the more I believe there is truth in this perception.

Something inexplicable was calling me forward to where I am now. I started with no clients, but I knew more people needed people like me. I had no product, but I knew I could teach and build a curriculum. I had no real plan other than being willing to build it and listen to others as I went along. Yes, I jumped into a fire, but looking back, I see myself leaving a safe and secure place with a long history and loyal colleagues to move into a dream calling out to me. Doing so broke ties with hundreds of people I loved, many of whom did not understand why I chose to move into the deep and cold waters of the unknown. I chose to take a perilous flight to the future and closing my eyes, I walked to a ledge and stepped off with my arms spread wide, trusting the wind would deposit me safely at the base of the mountain, ready to ascend the peaks once more.

When I look back now it is hard to imagine how we did it, hard to reason with how I mentally moved through it. Risk is where most people get stuck. Knowing I am not the kind to take risks and knowing I took an unsurmountable risk and gambled has me cringing in hindsight. My subconscious had to take the wheel. Deep inside, I allowed my calling to take the wheel, closed my conscious and pragmatic thinking to swim blindly toward the lighthouse beaconing in the distance.

I have written about this swim in my other book *Win or Learn*. It was a lonely, long, cold swim to a new shore, and reaching the shore was a no-fail option. I knew I had the strength to finish the swim. I knew my fuel was big enough to carry me to safety, even if the new land was a land of unknown and even if I had to live in the present moment day-by-day for a long time. I trusted my ability to go where my heart told me to go.

I am the worst financial investment client you will ever want to meet. I have an abnormal disdain for losses, and as I write this, the stocks and bonds I have invested in (because I am moderately positioned) are taking a bath. I hate losing hard-earned money, and I contemplate taking it all out daily, paying the penalties, and burying it all in mason jars in the backyard. Instead, I stay invested and seek reassurance from my exceptionally patient portfolio manager who has told me at least fifty times how the bond market works and schooled patience.

I have opened new legs of my firm after years of planning. These measures of new financial investment and risk-taking require careful, well-thought-out planning and repeated answering by the team I am entrusting to the new businesses. Still, I open new sales funnels, knowing at a higher level than my subconscious fears and desire to play it safe is the wise thing to do.

What are you playing too safe? What risk could you take which would return a more significant profit, greater happiness, or greater peace in your life? Learning to be a risk taker requires unlearning. I live the life of a risk taker in the body of a conservative. Mind over matter is indeed the power of mind steering us to greater heights even when our natural wiring says no. You can do this, if you choose.

Finding my path to honor has taken careful thinking and sometimes simple action-taking. I have mastered the skill of leaping into a crevice I believe will take me to the next peak on the mountain.

Are you willing to climb past your fears? Are you ready to blindly trudge ahead on faith and intuition, beliefs and pragmatic risk-taking? Would you get to new heights if you could move past where you are right now? Will you do it?

These questions are for you to answer and discuss with those who love you and whom you trust to provide guidance in your life. My life has evolved and reached incredible heights because of my ability to move and keep it moving forward. I promise you the view from each peak is spectacular.

*CHAPTER 10*

# Forgiving Your Killers

How many times in your life have you let someone kill you? Internally, mentally, philosophically, not physically, obviously. How often have you been slain by a friend, family member, co-worker, boss, or subordinate? How many times have you died at the hand of harsh and cruel words projected towards you by broken people who have not yet found salvation or self-worth? Hundreds of thousands of times in my life, I have felt hurt and harmed mentally, crushed at times even by someone who has callously spewed vitriol in my direction.

The verbal attacker, the below-the-belt defender, and the cold-hearted killer are all out there living amongst us. At some point in my life, I manufactured killers. Because of my strong-minded and outspoken ways, I have pulled otherwise quiet individuals out of the dark backgrounds into the fight to stand in conflict with me because I have unknowingly triggered their defense systems. And let's not even get started about the Alpha and as my good friend Jay Doran says, Fake Alphas. These are the most brutal of fighters as one is an auto-response, and you never realize you have tripped a wire until you find yourself toe-to-toe with one.

The Fake Alpha is typically one where you have to control your own Alpha to avoid causing a hanging in the town square resulting only in you appearing as the villain. These people are fun. The ones who throw punches because they genuinely believe they can fight and come at you with an inept argument, often ignorant and absent of factual data, just wailing their hands in the air trying to make contact.

For me, my Alpha comes with martial arts. I will slay when someone tires, trips, or simply fails to execute their point. I will take on the fight, bury them when I am done, and walk away unaffected by the kill.

I believe I am a stone-cold killer regarding words, protecting my integrity, and defending my loyal friends, family, and things I hold in the highest regard. I will slay sinners today whom I know need to be brought to their knees to make them a spectacle in the arena of onlookers if they dare come at me wrongly.

Let me be clear. I am not someone roaming around the world looking for conflict, and I am not someone seeking discord or even sniffing for it. I find myself emotionally exhausted after a confrontation, especially those emotionally evoked, as I have only one speed. KILL. Learning this about myself was a long process.

I felt guilty as a child about my Alpha, and I didn't even know why or what it was. I found myself slaying friends or turning on so-called friends when an interaction triggered my radar, and I was left feeling embarrassed and guilty. I had to learn over time to control myself. I had to learn to curb my appetite for blood when my eyes grew red.

For a long time, I examined the inner workings of my mind. I have asked myself who I am, what I am, and why I am what I am. The answers never come quickly for me. Instead, a clear understanding has slowly become focused while living my life. This clarity has helped me accept it's my nature to lead, to fight for good causes, to be the man of the people, to be the backbone for my family, and to help others less knowing learn through their journey in life.

I unveiled who I am long ago. Speaking about the truths I've learned is current and a bit raw in its newness. Labeling these truths of who I am? I avoided labels most of my life out of fear of self-loathing or ridicule, both of which were prevalent in my world. I have crossed the bridge from the mindset of giving a shit to take me as I am.

I found peace on the other side of this bridge. I found true friendships, genuine friendships. I found many people who did not cross the bridge with me, still living on the land of bullshit side of the bridge. Not my bullshit, theirs. Bullshit they tell themselves. Bullshit they tell others. Mounds and mounds of complete and utter bullshit.

There are also those playing it safe who live under the bridge and put themselves in the say yes to everything mindset. Men and women who profess they will love everyone, cause no disruption and say yes to everything. These are honestly indifferent people who are existing in the world. I am perplexed by these people, by the way. They wake, go to a job they dislike, and return at the end of the day to a house not a home. How sad it is to live in dysfunction, just existing. They pay their taxes, mow their lawns, go to school functions, and water their plants, all while staying under the radar. Theirs is a choice to NOT make moves causing attention. It is their desire to stay in the norm, not seek excitement, simply remain within the margins of their lives wishing only to stay out of harm, avoiding mindsets they consider to be nonsense and fools and the all-knowing truth givers and seekers.

They are waiting to die. I am fine with this so long as they replace the resources they use. Show me a hardworking person living under the bridge who is essentially a good person, and I will happily invite them to my world to dwell where they are most comfortable. Under-the-bridge dwellers are often reliable if unimaginative worker bees.

Over on the bullshit side of the bridge are the cheating husbands, lying wives, thieves, and cheaters in life, robbing employers of resources, and minutes of time, and cutting corners. They talk about their friends, put people down for the same damn shit they do every day, and go along with the trends and the masses. They're also probably paying their taxes, yet they are extroverts leading small packs of mindless soldiers. Bullshit Land! Like Candy Land without ladders and chutes.

I have lived on the bullshit side and been an active participant a good part of my life. I have committed all the crimes listed, both knowingly and unknowingly. I bought into my own bullshit for so long and was in so deep, I could not see who I was.

It is hard to get out of Bullshit Land because nobody is going to tell you the truth about where you are living. Half of your friends don't know it themselves, and the other half know and don't want to leave.

What caused me to see the bullshit was a break in a deep friendship. A friend who had grown greedy robbed me of resources, shook the foundation of my loyalty, and allowed me to wake up and see the church I prayed to was a mirage.

In the end, this person did me an enormous favor. I am at peace with this individual today, beyond the hate and emotional tsunami I lived with for many years. I let it all go when I crossed the bridge to the truth.

Today I am proud, not ashamed, of who I am. I vividly understand my flaws and have learned difficult lessons the hard way. Through losing loved ones, titles, fame, and fortune, and rebuilding myself a few times, I realize most of my heartache has been my own fault. As a result of repeatedly hurting myself, eventually, I survived.

When I sat in the audience in Philadelphia to see Jay Doran's Liar Lid speech, I was amazed. Resonate is not a strong enough word to describe how fully I related to his story and writings. I knew I must undertake my journey, as he had, to shed the layers of fake and materialistic existence I was living and become rebirthed as the person God put me on this earth to be.

Before I met Jay, I was on the path I had fought to walk. My journey was underway and let me be clear, I did good. My life is not a sad, sappy story of total loss. It's a story of early struggle brought on by economic deficit. It's the story of repeatedly overcoming and falling from grace due to depression and emotions I could not control or process. I was physically drawn to the fire and lacked the vital self-control to resist the flames despite considering myself an intelligent human. The mirror I held to my face showed a false image. I denied visible facts which, had I looked throughout my life, were feeding a physical hunger.

Mine has been a life with goodness searching for how to make it great. Many of us fall victim to a similar life. In my view, it's no longer acceptable to be like mainstream when the mainstream is bad.

Today I am living free of sin. I mean, I am not purposely or consciously sinning. I am sure there is always room for me to grow. Today I respect my body and soul for the power they had to steer the ship regardless of my mind. I try even today to appreciate the command of not gossiping and enjoy the greater self-worth this choice brings. We all know gossiping is useless and wrong. Still, many of us can't help ourselves. I debate this in my mind as I know venting about the stupid, ignorant guy at work is cathartic and necessary. However, I follow the rule of only talking about others if you stand to help or heal yourself or someone else. When I relegate any talk of others to this rule, the language sounds different, and so does the resulting action.

I had to look back over the bridge and forgive my killers. A few folks had life sentences in my mind, and I shocked myself when I forgave them too. I remember how it felt to let the hurt and heartache in my mind go. Even when they didn't deserve forgiveness, even when they were guilty of their crimes against me, I forgave and gained from forgiving. It made me think honestly about the guys I had put to death. I laugh saying this out loud. I am pretty sure I killed some people in my mind, theoretically. I don't mean I dreamed of killing them, either. I mean to me, they were dead, nonexistent. Their wrong-doings were too deep in my mind to ever heal my wounds. Or are they? I wonder if, in my lifetime, I will resurrect those dead bodies in my mind's eye? Whether I will let myself think of the person I cast away forever? I really don't know. I only know I keep surprising myself.

Forgiving your killers is a whole psychological sport. One I knew deep inside was necessary and beneficial, but stubbornness in me would not permit it. Until all damage was done and all hope of reconciliation was lost, I refused to contemplate forgiveness.

My reluctance to forgive is a contradiction to my faith base and commitment to the Bible which clearly teaches forgive all even thine enemy. Those words rang in the subconscious of my mind without action until one day I allowed myself to consciously recognize my goodness internally was begging me to be the person I was born to be, let go of the hurt and harm done to me by others, and look harder at what part I played in the situation. It won't surprise anyone to learn when I looked, I found mistakes I had made and breaks I had provoked, and damage I had done. My role was additive or even a catalyst to the collision.

Knowing I was a contributor to my hurt or harm was a revelation. I remember the moment I felt it and thought it, the villain became less important in my head's story. I realized I WAS going to be able to forgive my killers after all. The ball began rolling then and there.

After finishing the self-work, I found the concept of forgiving less daunting. Once the role of the killer was undramatized and re-aligned with its reality, I could see clearly. When the complete picture came into play, I could try to understand the violence towards me, whether verbal, physical, or mental. ONLY then did I understand fully the crime committed had an accomplice—Me!

When I sat with my killers in my mind, the crime was clear to me, and an appropriate penalty became possible. I was able to say, "I forgive you" to the killer in my mind and approve release for time served. I could even add the killer to my prayers and instead of wishing them ill will in my angry mind as I had done for so long, I was able to say, this soul needs saving.

The moment my forgiveness became real and tangible, my heart opened and let the light in, and everything for me changed. I learned I am a loving person but when met with harsh treatment, an explosive defense autopilot takes me on a path to war, if the cut us deep enough. The deeper the cut the longer the war.

I learned the tragedy of my wars was often self-inflicted wounds brought on by the flailing around of my arms in a fit of rage.

Anger has its place, but when displayed is never seen as being in control or emotionally intelligent. Because I show intense anger when hurt, others see me as less, or lacking, or emotional. Knowledge of these false views killed me internally for many years. I wanted approval, yet I had to succumb to who I was.

Over time I discovered a need for people like me in the world. I am the person who will say what others won't, who will stick with the mission to its end, who will fight off the worst of evil and save the most people. I have joined the forces of those at war. I know people trust me because being honest means being trustworthy.

Once I forgave my killers, I immediately felt less anxiety, more happiness, and better self-love. These effects are not cliché fodder, but rather a return on the investment of my forgiveness in a real, visible, and meaningful way.

Do you want more happiness and less anxiety? If your answer is yes, put in the work I outline, and I promise you will thank me for the rest of your life. I was fortunate enough to receive this advice from Jay and worked on dissecting its

many parts. Had I not been led in this direction; I promise you I would not have ended up experiencing the peace and happiness I now relish every single day. I lived for too long in my own prison. I had no idea I had the key in my pocket the whole time.

Finally, and foremost, I want you to know even though I forgave my killers, I never let them back into my world. I kept them on castaway island. Don't let my choice in this influence your choice. My path to forgiveness didn't come with permission to re-enter my world. I am smart enough to know I can change myself, but also smart enough to know when I should believe a person who shows who they are. The odds of being re-traumatized by the same person is highly likely if we don't create healthy boundaries. Consider this in your journey. We can recover from people, but we don't always have to reunite with them.

*CHAPTER 11*

# Guilty as Charged

We committed a crime. By we, I mean you or me, one of us, or all of us, at some time or another, commits a sin or literal crime by the standards of moral justice or law. We get away with it. Yippee! We move on. What is the price tag? Did we win? Are we relieved, or does an inner voice embedded deep down inside speak to our subconscious saying, "You are not nice. You are not good. What you did is wrong. You shouldn't have done that. Why did you do that?" Insert dramatic music and bad feelings here.

Most humans grapple with the picture I am painting. The Ten Commandments we are raised by measure the lies, omissions, and acts of deceit, intentional or unintentional. If you were not raised under Christianity, look to your list, every religion has one. We share universal truths as humans. Each of us has a moral code telling us we did wrong, and wrongdoing at all levels comes with a price tag impacting our physical and mental wellness.

I am sorry to be the party pooper who brings up this topic. I was taught right from wrong according to my parents' ethics, and they were taught right from wrong by their parents' ethics. It is likely your moral ethics spring from the same font. And yet, more matters in life than our learned ethics. Our internal human wiring is hardwired and comes with no explanation or lessons provided. Nowhere in our scholastic journey does someone sit down and talk about how our body reacts and the physical and mental toll it takes to perform acts of delinquency. No one warns us about our internal code, which will psychologically damn us.

Sure, we have seen the crime shows where guilt drives a person to confess their sins or crimes. In Hollywood movies, we see malicious acts committed by the haunted person who then verbally outs their deceit by coming clean, if you will. These are dramatic representations of what I am speaking of here, our internal code.

We are born with our moral code. Our code can be loud, and it can grow impossible to ignore if we look even slightly in its direction. Once we become consciously aware of the internal angst we feel over a situation, the rabbit is out of the hat. There is no putting it back.

Are you thinking about how your conscious wiring is laid out? If you are someone who can sin without major guilt, and who can thieve without being plagued by it, I would argue your journey is the farthest because, for whatever reason, you aren't even on the road to salvation yet, and are likely to be a repeat offender.

Guilty as Charged, the title of this chapter implies we ARE guilty the moment we commit the act. Most of us feel guilty even if we aren't caught doing something wrong. Denial of the code is disrupted immediately by getting caught. Being caught, even by self-discovery, often leads to a self-loathing implosion. A cheater for instance will feel incredible shame if caught by a spouse or friend when being deceitful because at our core, we all recognize wrong acts, and how they reflect poor character.

We can't deny the code. We can't operate in complete denial of it because part of life's journey is listening to our internal wiring and aligning our actions with the code. It is by aligning ourselves with our code, we can love ourselves.

And herein lies the premise of this book. I was on a liar's path for a long time in my life. Does this mean the single acts of deceit or lying which could have occurred at different intersections define my life's work or action? Not at all. It means I had not yet embraced the possibility of finding answers in my psyche. I already had the answers to freeing myself and loving myself wholly. The day I understood this was the day I realized people who sin self-medicate. People going against their code often suffer from some form of external dulling to the consciousness through alcohol or drug abuse or mental illness. One of these three is usually in play.

Rarely do you see a person involved in a blatant affair who is not internally conflicted. Actions driven by lust include knowing its mere existence is flawed. I am not using cheating on a spouse as the example because I cheated, or someone cheated on me although both of those statements are true in my lifetime. It isn't the most prevalent of crimes I feel I committed; it simply is the easiest and most relatable one to teach most humans.

Guilty as charged is about whether you charge yourself with the crime. If you do not, I assume a justification is occurring in your mind's eye.

We often hear voices of reason in our heads which aren't reasonable. "She's a bitch, and I deserve better treatment," or "He is emotionally closed off, and I deserve praise and intimacy from a man." What those voices should say is, "It is wrong to do that" or "Don't do it."

No matter how sad, sorry, lonely, or neglected we are, the proper choice is to move past the temptation, deny the physical desire, stay faithful to your partner and relationship. If you have a problem, stop it today, and when you overcome issues, use your experience to teach others how they can do the same.

What do I want to accomplish with *Finding Honor* the book? I want us to realize the journey to self-love and ultimate salvation is complex and hard, realize when we are born, we are given all we need to be the very best version of ourselves. It is a matter of listening to the code inside us and honoring it.

Honor the code. Find Your Honor. It's already there waiting for you in your most natural state. Listen. Be conscious of and live in your moral code. Don't deny yourself the inner voice to protect the kingdom of our spirit. We are our own gods in many ways. We either live and die by the code or wobble and weave around it.

When I decided to honor my set of principals not to lie, to be as honest as I could be, to not gossip, to live a pure life and to give back, to drive to good places, to give of myself and my gift, the world completely and inexplicably opened up for me. Finding honor HAS been a long journey. My steps have not all been right. My denial of wrongdoing has been strong at times. Experiences I felt were special and denying my inner code's warnings almost killed me several times. I sank into deep depressions, self-medicated, and was angry for long periods of times. I isolated, something few people know about me, but vividly true for many years. I simply disappeared. People ask me when and I can say 1991, 1997 and 1998, also in 2000 I was secluded. Later I would do so again in 2016, only showing up for work but not socializing or visiting anyone and spending every free moment alone and inside. I believe during those years I was fighting my code, and by giving in to it, I redirected and found my way back to honor.

Changing this behavior is not a once-and-done journey. I would reach a place where I could return to happiness and honor, only to take the wrong roads again. I will share more about those dark places in the latter chapters of this book. It may shock those who read it but I had to truly fight for my life in Finding my Honor. I am here today as your teacher to say you can do it too.

I believe at any time in our lives we can be in some form of this battle, and we can be on the losing or winning side of it. I don't know where this book finds you right now or how much of what I share resonates with your internal code. But I believe if you are present and aware while reading this, if you are willing to look yourself in the mirror, the first step will lead to the next and inexorably to the next.

As you embark on this journey, it is vital you find a good counselor or a good and dear loyal friend to speak your egregious errors aloud truthfully. It is crucial to the healing journey and your conscious acceptance to recognize your faults, your sins, and your crimes.

Criminals stay behind bars until they admit their crimes. I know firsthand because the murderer of my dear friend Nikki Evangelous comes up for parole every year and attempts to justify his actions, and every year the parole board denies his freedom. I firmly believe this is because he has not admitted his wrongdoing. He can't repent what he does not acknowledge and own, and because he won't admit, he is not recovered or healed in the court's eyes and thus not rehabilitated. Even the legal system of this century still follows this psychological code of ethics and human science. One cannot move to a place of healing and honor until one does the work described in this book.

Finding honor is a journey to dark places and beyond. You cannot find the light until you face the dark first. There are no shortcuts. I promise you this as I tried every shortcut possible and denied myself true healing for decades. There is no other medical cure except this path I describe and know to be the journey to salvation.

I realize this may sound biblical in its writing. Without intending it to be religious, I believe using characters, and historical figures from the Bible helps describe our internal code in its crime versus punishment system.

Religion generally speaks of justice as being carried out against those caught. This book speaks of justice served internally. There is no docket to stand before, and no jury or judge to convince. In this book, you mete out justice by doing the work.

When we fall ill and can't find the physical reason, we should look to our mental wellness. Our psyche influences our health and is driven by our moral code and barometer. The effects of following your code and internal barometer are hefty. We see it every day.

I wrote this book for myself and you because we all are born sinners. If you read this and can't relate to this statement, perhaps you are living a wholesome life by the standards you measure. The lessons in *Finding Honor* are meant to share and carry to others who need it. I promise you need not look far to find those who need and are ready to embrace finding honor. Your children will need this lesson one day. You may have a sibling or even a struggling parent. This lesson could guide them to salvation.

What if you could give people true happiness? Peace? Would you be willing to be the hero in their story? How much honor do you have in yourself to be the person who helps others find it? Will it be you or will you be the messenger?

We should all act. This is God's work.

# CHAPTER 12

# No Goodbyes

In 1986 I was driving my mother's Ford Granada. I had just earned my license and I was picking up a dear friend and high school buddy to head over to a party in Bristol, one town over. I remember how hard we laughed that night when we broke the bench seat in my parents' car.

At first, we heard it but could not figure out what it was. The leg went straight though the bottom of the rusted-out floor causing sparks to fly and this horrid metal on pavement sound. We kept looking in the rear-view mirror and twice we pulled over to check if the muffler had fallen loose and was scraping as we drove down the highway, but neither time could we see what was scraping beneath the car.

It was not until the leg broke straight through from the weight of my big buddy that we realized what had happened and laughed hysterically. Tears streamed down my face as we laughed. My head was squished to the roof of the car while he sat low, barely able to see out the side window. We propped the seat up and kept going.

The next day, when my folks headed to buy groceries, they sat in the seat, and the leg again broke through the floor, leaving them in the same position but thinking it was a new occurrence. For many years, they remained unaware my friend and I had broken it first.

It was incredibly funny both to experience and to witness. This is one of many stories I could share about my friend. I will purposely not share his name because I cannot ask permission to use his name in the real story I will share in this chapter. The story is not harsh or defaming to anyone. It is a story about love and friendship. Make no mistake, it is also a sad story with a sad ending.

I am sharing because as this story unfolded, I was tested to my core in a way I have never been tested before. The lessons from this experience helped shape my honor and this book is about unearthing the lessons and sharing my journey.

This book would be incomplete without me writing this chapter. And while I may never expand this chapter in and of itself out of fear of controversy, I will honor myself and my friend by sharing it.

The years rolled on for my friend and me. We both went off to college, met significant others and married, attended each other's weddings, stayed in touch, and visited when we could. We both had one child. We were happy adults.

However, our lives though were not without tragedy. My friend lost his father to a murder. He came to me with his inheritance looking for financial advice to buy a home which was my profession, asking if I would assist. We were riding along in life, growing and aging.

We were lifelong friends. My oldest memory of him is in the first grade when he stood before the class and proclaimed he was from Mars. How we laughed; even the teacher. This was his humor; it was his core and superpower. Our whole lives, we laughed and laughed.

Eventually our interactions were fewer and further between. Still, when we had the rare occasion to reunite at a wedding or, sadly, a funeral, we picked up where we left off and spent all the hours we could together. How I loved his laugh and his jokes and his smile. That never changed for me.

My friend was diagnosed with Crohn's disease and his battle was mighty and long. He eventually lost his battle and passed away a year ago. As sad and heartbreaking as his ending was, it's in the days leading to the end of his life when the greatest tragedy for me occurred.

After his diagnosis, I spoke to him about a mutual friend who had Chron's disease, and we saw each other at our friend's funeral. Soon after I learned he was so sick his imminent demise was near. I read a social post and realized he was doing some sort of goodbye tour and of course I immediately reached out. He was slow to respond, and I chalked it up to his being sick.

I saw the posts reporting the goodbye lunches and yet he never really answered about seeing me. In one of the posts, a girl appeared whom I had gone to school with and whose brother I had dated and broken up with. She was not a fan of mine, and I was indifferent to her. I saw a picture of her with my friend on the goodbye lunch tour, and I admit it stung me. I knew in my lifetime, although it was not a competition,

I had been closer to him than she had. I remember seeing the picture motivated me to reach out and again no answer came back.

I felt desperate to find out why he suddenly was not returning my texts or messages. I asked a mutual friend to ask, and eventually, the message came back saying my friend had no intention of seeing me. The message came with no explanation. I remember as the days and weeks rolled on my angst rose and I lay awake at night searching for why he would not want to see me to say our farewells.

I went back over and accounted for everything I had said and written. My mutual friend who I had leaned on for advice visited him again and was told my friend had received a curt text from me. I reflected and remembered writing an angry text asking what on earth was happening.

I didn't regret writing it as I deserved more than no response. I cried out of embarrassment and shame, our friends were seeing him and rallying around him, and I so wanted to wrap myself around him too. It would never happen.

Over time I accepted this slight. Many of my closest friends spoke with him; I suffered through his death and funeral (not attending) alone. Many months would pass before I came to understand. I realize he believed I had changed. I recall him jokingly calling me Tony Robbins. My profession of course in professional development had hues of inspiring and motivating speeches and lectures. I realized, in hindsight, he was shaming me over my life choices. I realized in the end he had grown to dislike me, or perhaps was not able to accept the career choices and successes I experienced.

It is the only explanation I have come to, and reality is harsher than anything I have ever felt in my life. His actions of dying without speaking to me over a perceived change in who I had become were cruel. A lifelong friend delivered the greatest level of disdain anyone has ever pointed at me in such a severe way.

I was told he didn't want drama while he was dying. I know this was an excuse. I hadn't brought him drama and in fact, I brought him care and love. I had a logical and fair question as to why he had been overlooking me for his farewell tour. I suspect his closeness to my ex-boyfriend's sister was also at play.

In the end, I found knowing his reasons didn't provide me satisfaction or closure, but it did challenge my courage. Had I been in any other place or time in my life when I was less steadfast in my internal belief system, I would have been more than shaken, I would have been destroyed.

Not to minimize the effects of this tragic ending to a lifelong friendship, I was devastated in all the ways one can measure devastation. I cried endlessly grieving for an entire year, awkwardly, uncontrollably. One day without notice I stopped crying and realized I was moving through the grief. This occurred while he was still alive but near death.

His eventual death was a period at the end of a long process and story for me. I knew there would be more pain to endure when I chose not to attend his funeral. I felt the shame of other's judgment, who may or may not have known why I didn't appear at his funeral. I suspected much would be said to and from my friends and yet I was able to live with it all and dismiss its sting.

In my heart of hearts, I knew the punishment doled out to me for a harsh text would have been more regretted by me had I not stated my truth. I also came to terms with his character, sick or not, to accept this was on him not me.

I was able to stay true to myself throughout and stay honorable. When his birthday came and went, I said Happy Birthday on social media along with his friends. When his anniversary came, I said Happy Anniversary as well. I texted his wife, who I love and respect, to offer my love and concern. Those messages were ignored as well.

I finally stopped sending messages shortly after his passing. I know he saw my texts during his final year. He died knowing I loved him. And he died knowing his choice to ignore me would go to his death and I wondered how that made him feel. I wondered what it was like to have such anger towards someone who had never shown anything but love to him his whole life.

I was still whole. I was still who I had always been, and this event didn't change me. The act of omission didn't rob me. It opened my eyes and made me see who was and was not in my corner. It made me see other people moving through this situation positioning. I made a mental list of who I could trust and who would no longer fool me.

Success sometimes has a price tag. Peoples' journey towards success will leave friends on the road behind or choosing to get off. Many a spouse, peer, colleague, or friend has become jealous of our growth they cannot share. I have seen it with my own eyes and now experienced it in the worse of ways.

The days leading to his death were not completely broken. I chose honor. I chose love. While he didn't text or call me, I sent him love notes. I sent him three-word texts like I love you, and thinking of you, once a month.

Luckily, three days prior to his passing I sent my final message not giving in to the anger and hurt I felt inside, I honored who I was. He died knowing who I ultimately am. And in the end, he didn't control the outcome and make me hate or angry or become the martyr. He owned the martyr spot in this story, and he died the antagonist in my world, not I. Nobody can re-write this story without my perspective because nobody but me had to choose love and honor over hate and anger towards him.

On the day his life was celebrated I gave my well wishes to a dear friend who was attending. He knew how I felt. I was mad inside still, yet I managed to stay at peace.

I won't visit his grave because I speak to him through my mind's eye and prayer. In my head and heart, he knows where I stand and to honor myself, I will not share those thoughts or words with anyone. If there is an afterlife, and if people can hear you speak to them in prayer as we have come to believe here on earth, then he knows how I feel. He knows how he affected me and how his final decisions affect me and his loss. He knows my heart, and he knows how wrong he was to think even for a moment I wasn't one of his dearest of friends. These truths and sentiments have been put to God and prayer and sent into the universe. I didn't need to see him to believe the message reached its destination either, as my faith is as strong as any human on this planet or any other planet. My faith has shown me its power throughout my life. I gave this moment to my faith and it is what will carry me onward.

Sometimes there are No Goodbyes, and sometimes we have to live with a sudden departure, unexpected or expected. In tragedy, we must learn to live with honor of that person and ourselves and it can be conventionally and traditionally done, or through means of faithful speak. If you reflect on my first chapter, Premonitions and Recurring Dreams, you already know talking to the dead for me is not a one-time occurrence; call it what you want. I have mastered the No Goodbye of this human world. I have found honor in leaning into my internal belief systems.

When your belief is real, and your self-love is real, you can find the honor you deserve. I am an honorable human. I live by a code of ethics I would put up against most people and believe I would come out the victor.

You can live past the No Goodbye and process a proper ending with the tools of faith and prayer, self-talk, and reflection. Choose love, forgiveness, and honor. I stayed true to myself through this process and was given one of the greatest gifts rising out of one of the most painful times and circumstances. God has lessons for us, and he used this moment in time to teach me. It is a blessing wrapped inside of pain. I found the prize in pain.

# CHAPTER 13

# The Heartbreak Toll

How much are you willing to pay for love? I wonder if we were to ask every human who was falling in love, would we ever hear someone answer, my life? Would you risk your life for love? I know many of you will say yes to this. Maybe you think of your children and of course I would throw myself in front of a moving train for my kid. What I mean here is the kind of love we feel intimately with another human when entering a relationship. Would you risk your life for it?

There is a toll, a risk we all take by allowing ourselves to be loved and be in relationships. We open ourselves up to the vulnerability of giving our lives and hearts to someone else. Sometimes we build families and businesses around love, so when the love comes crumbling down, we must figure out if we can put the pieces back together, and most of the time, we can't. Not the same way anyways. The shattered vision in our minds of the dreams we held in love will destroy our confidence and embitter us to the sweetness of life, often taking down families and businesses in the domino effects of its cruelty.

And then there are serial daters who seem to be in love with being in love. Maybe they love the chase? I know of men who loved to chase but lost their passion once they caught their prey. Sound familiar? Are you the hunter or the prey? I am asking because which of the two types of people you relate to depends on who you relate to in this analogy.

If you relate to being the prey, then, of course, you have been chased by someone who enjoyed the game of love. Millions of people love courtship; women and men alike and on both sides of the love isle. When love runs its course and love's bottom begins to leak and slowly drain to the bottom of its barrel, what does it look like for the empath? How does the one left behind feel when the person who moved on has left?

I debated including this chapter partly because the stories are super personal and not all my own. The journey to honor builds on truth. And my story or not, these are truths deserving of being shared.

As I write this, I am anguished and riddled with internal strife and excruciating pain. Raw empathic emotion is threatening to take me under this transferred empathetic pain of loss is not directly my own. My elder sister is in hospice dying from a broken heart and she is losing her battle. I have seen how love can destroy us.

The loss of my sister's marriage is not my story to tell. She was not ready for it to end; its ending sent her into depression. Depression has slowly but surely robbed her of joy in her life.

Ripping joy out of her heart has left her lonely. Loneliness and worry have made her sick. Sickness drove her to the darkest of dark places, and that place is destroying her. Out of respect for her I will not give intimate details of her demise. Suffice it to say her declining physical health and mental wellness is on a downward spiral we cannot stop. All I can do is to be there for her.

Love can destroy us. I have experienced it. I too have been destroyed by losing love. I have been shattered inside after being left by someone I love. I learned the hard way to respect the power of love and love lost.

I remember the first time I was devastated by someone moving on from me. I was a teenager, and the pain felt like nothing I had ever felt. I thought life as I knew it had ended, and I mourned its loss as deeply as one might a physical death. Crying and sick, I took to my bed, where I dwelled on loss and lamented over it for a long time until my mother literally kicked my butt out of bed and told me to get going.

She ultimately saved me from a long and bitter battle that would have taken me to much darker places, although I did not know it then. Later in life, when I was left on my own to recover from similar situations, I could not see the early signs or stop the spiral into darkness. Those bottoms, for me, were deeper and more profound than most people could imagine.

I have never said what I am about to say, and while I fear judgment by writing these words, it's time. Twice in my life I have been hospitalized for clinical depression. Both times the onset was the heartache of love lost and broken. Both times I was left to pick up the pieces of a life I had imagined and a path I was walking. It was impossible at the time for me to take steps to start over and I obsessively dwelled on the belief I could save the relationship.

I am a stubborn person, and it is a trait I know has helped me persevere well past the miles of a typical mountain climber. My mind has been pushing my body my whole life. When that push is flipped upside down it drives to dark places and down dead-end roads. The almighty strength of stubbornness, blanketed by a blind spot in logical thinking brought on by a denial factor, ends up far down bad paths and leads to dismal places.

Admitting this weakness is still embarrassing to me. Even though I have completed much work in this area of my life to prevent reaching those depths again, I know with certainty I could end up there again. Once we know the bottomless pit of despair and take the ride to its true depths, we never walk a path in this life without remembered knowledge of the dark pathways. I know what others are thinking when they choose to take their life, for instance. I see what others feel when they curl up in a ball and are all consumed by the pain of heartache.

The toll of loving is priceless and infinite. There is no way to name its price; it costs everything and nothing at the same time. It's both the best and worst investment you will ever make, enriching and depleting, fuel and deterrent. We open ourselves up to the vulnerability of giving our lives and hearts to someone else. We build families and businesses around love and when love comes crumbling down, we have to figure out how to put the pieces back together. Love is a feeling not to be played with or ignored because it is almighty in its force. We can't protect ourselves against love or imagine a life where love doesn't have a negative connotation equally as much as it infers pleasure.

Love is the red crayon heart symbol I wrote on my fourth-grade English paper when asked what makes the world go around. Love is the same red crayon heart scribbled on a blank piece of paper my 9-year-old self proudly displayed to a laughing little boy I had a crush on. Love is this story told so many times by me in my life, only to question myself later and left feeling vulnerable and dumb. I hated the choice my young self-made declaring love as my universal language, and yet, it is still what I believe is the greatest gift.

Love is incredible in its power and reach. Love has shown me it can span past a physical break. Long after a relationship has ended, I still love some people, even though everything logically stands to tell me to be wise and to let go or stop loving; it endures. It endures because once found, it is truly unconditional. Love is a fuel whose light never extinguishes or fades when in its purest form.

I have also closed the door on love I ultimately realized was not true. For many years, I lived on a path with someone I thought I loved and didn't, someone whose heart I broke in the end.

It's happened not with one person but many. I realize I have sought relationships for the wrong reasons. Out of loneliness, for example, I compromised my internal barometer and simply filled a seat with someone who would become my life companion for a while. Love is amazing. My heart sought more than what I had given it, as if it knew I was not drinking from the most intoxicating kind of love there could be.

When I assess the personal damage I put on others in my quest for true love, I regret those intersections in my younger years. I hurt people who deserved more than I gave them in the end. I left more than one person destroyed by my departure, and in a few instances, my departure was abrupt and sudden.

Walking away and not revisiting those relationships in my mind was easy. I hate to report this, but it's true. I understand now I had loved but not been in love. I am unsure which one of those two kinds of loves are better for me. Having love was a companionship which felt lesser and eventually non-satisfying. Being in love was all intense and unconditional. It felt scary and powerful, distracting and consuming.

I also believe I don't do love well. I am nervous when I am in genuine love. I am worried about it ending, about my vulnerability, about losing it. I once ended a long-term relationship, one of the truest of loves I had felt to that point in my life, because of a physical attraction I felt for someone else. Not because I thought I would have a better life with the other person but because I felt it was wrong to have the feelings.

I now know those feelings would have passed if I had maintained my relationship. Eventually, I would have overcome the short-lived feelings and my real love for my mate would survive those fleeting emotions. Ultimately, I made a grave decision which took me to my knees after the breakup and kept me there for years.

I masked my heartache over that time with drugs and alcohol to numb the pain always lingering in the background of my life. I was able to work and function but barely. When I ultimately sought help, counseling, discovery, and repair, I came to terms with my inability to put the pieces back together.

I stepped out onto a new path to begin again, forever changed. It was as if a door in my life had been nailed shut, never to be opened again, the key thrown away, and the lock seared shut.

How would I go forward? Could I ever love again? These are questions I've been answering for the better part of two decades now. I have moved on, and I have found love again. I won't label the love I have other than to say it is one of mutual respect with a person of great character, who lived through many years of my sadness and illness and stayed by my side;

it's a loyal and healthy love and one I admire greatly. It is love, there is no doubt.

The person I am today is closed off from the dark place I went, the place that stood to kill me. My penance, the toll I've paid for love, is my belief in the fairy tale. Everyone does not remain in a fairy tale love forever. They don't. We don't. I didn't. Fairy tales are for kids, and anyone who says their life is a fairy tale is living in an incomplete book and should consider what chapter of their life they are in.

There is nothing cynical in this depiction or belief. All love ends up broken, or it evolves and grows. This is not cynicism, rather a warning. Happy endings are for fairy tales. Love and life move past the fairy tale.

I hope there are more surprises for me with regard to my learning about love. I am settled in my long-term relationship; it is the longest relationship of my life and I wish for it not to change in any way. I look to the future and wonder what love I will feel in five or ten years? Will I grow to a place unknown to me that will make me whole again one day? Will I live to climb to the highest mountain top of a mythical place I once dreamed I could be where I loved myself as much as I obeyed the power of external love? That is the mission I am now on.

The toll of love is whatever price you put on it. The toll to not love is to have not lived knowing its power. There is beauty in knowing both.

# CHAPTER 14

# Finding the Door

Suddenly the storm clouds parted, the sun shone through, and the blue sky opened wide. We all know the moment when the dark finally passes and the beautiful light is let into our lives. Often, it happens without a major battle or fight; it's simply a storm cloud lifting after a downpour. The difference between bad weather and dark times in our life is dark times come to stay. They unpack themselves and move in often lasting for months, even years.

The dark times are the guest you can't get to leave. The guest who overstays their visit; unwanted and unrelenting. Except this kind of guest robs you of more than privacy, they steal your happiness, your peace and comfort, and often your sanity. This guest comes to keep you from healing your broken heart and brings punishment, blasting your inner empath with hurt and pain.

In my lifetime, I have endured this visitor many times. Sometimes I let it in, and other times the visitor showed up and let itself in unannounced and uninvited. Recognizing you are living in a dark time in your life is the first part of moving away from it and kicking the unwanted guest out. You are the person in control. It takes looking at the pain and looking at your darkness full on to recover.

We often go along to get along, keeping ourselves in pain and unrest because we refused to stand up for our own feelings. It's OK to not want a person in your life anymore. It's OK to not want to do something you don't like. It's OK to leave a job for no reason other than it's killing you, even when it is going to create financial hardship when the price tag is your ultimate happiness and peace. You do not need a reason to leave a relationship. As much as we always want to play the hero in our stories, we can break up with someone simply because we don't love them or think it's a dead end, as hard as that is to admit.

In short, STOP doing what you don't want or like. STOP. If you don't stop, you are giving away valuable time and rendering your happiness with it. What value do you put on these things? Why do we need to be angry to stand up for ourselves? Why do we wait for a reason when how we feel should dictate the reason, even if it's not logical?

I have had times in my life where I thought the storm would never pass and without fail every single time it ended when I let myself out. I was praying for better days ahead, I was working towards solutions, and I was doing my best to fix the problems. I was also lying to myself and everyone around me.

I was literally sitting feet from a door I could open and walk through. I did not open the door. Why wouldn't I open the door? For many reasons. A feeling of guilt. A feeling of failure. A feeling of not being finished, of wanting to leave in a caring way, not wanting to hurt anyone, and not knowing where I was going next. We don't act in our darkness for these reasons and more. The truth is, even the most prepared life doesn't follow its own plan. Having a plan for life is great but waiting to be inspired to rewrite the plan when it's gone wrong is a problem made tenfold worse when we are in the dark.

Today I am living in the light. During my last round of darkness, I think I was forever changed. I have been living in the light for six or seven years now and I hope it's my permanent location. Don't misunderstand, I am ever vigilant. Darkness has come knocking on my door. I know it's just outside my window, on the porch lurking. Waiting. I can see it peering in the window, ever ready to enter should I open the door.

I have decided it's a visitor I will meet on the steps of my life, not inside the door. This visitor is not welcome. I have decided I will not let the darkness in when I experience stress related to incidents or situations, including the death or sickness of a loved one. I have become the doorman of my psychological life. I choose when I let pain come in and sit with me, and I no longer let my free mind dwell. I am aware of how much time I spend talking about it.

I want to be clear here. I am not saying stuff the tough into a box in the corner. I am not saying to avoid pain. We must address our pain. I am saying confront what is coming to kill or hurt. Spend the necessary time with it and then like a pair of shoes, put it back on the shelf knowing you can take it back out anytime. From that point on in your day, week, or life you are going to shift gears and live your happy life.

I had a certified counselor teach me this and we made conscious decisions to talk about the painful issues in my life and we made conscious decisions to NOT talk about my pain but rather my happiness. I am sitting in the light of my life today and it is where you will find me 90 percent of the time. I do not sit in the dark anymore.

I wish I had let myself out of the darkness far sooner than I did. After one of my break ups from a long-term relationship, I chose to leave, and I put myself in a dark place. Internally, I knew I had hurt someone, and I knew in hurting them it made me feel bad inside. I didn't love myself for it and I also questioned my own motives. I had simply fallen out of love with this person and was unhappy. I had been living in that dark place a long time in my unhappiness and even after because I had no good reason to leave other than I wanted to.

Between the time I spent in darkness during the relationship and then after the breakup spiraling deeper into darkness, I slowly drifted into clinical depression. Like the metaphoric visitor we've been talking about, depression took hold and before I realized it; I was sleeping 16 hours a day, had lost 40 pounds, and was in poor mental and physical shape. Recognizing this was hard for me because I was in the woods of the darkness unable to see the trees for the forest, if you will. When others began to tell me they were concerned I realized my situation. Yet I was so deep in the darkness, calling for help took many more months after recognizing my situation.

Awareness is everything. You aren't on the path to the light until you become self-aware. I ask, as you are reading these words, would you do a mental health check with me?

Answer these rhetorical questions in your head. No need to write it down, this is an internal barometer check.

- Are you sleeping more than usual?
- Have you lost/gained a substantial amount of weight?
- Are you doing less socially?
- Do you find yourself removed from what normally brings you joy?
- Are you searching for help in your mind but not vocalizing it?
- Are you currently in a relationship you want to leave?
- Are you currently in a job you want to leave?
- Do you have someone in your life who is sick or dying?
- Are you sick or dying?
- Can you find the door?

So many of us are looking in all the wrong places for the answers to these questions. I would argue the journey to this truth is absolutely elusive. People who do not recognize their ability, or inability, to admit their issues, their driven deceit and their lack of boundaries or control, cannot find the truth or the cure.

Many a good man will be taken down by denial. I know of many people dying a slow but certain death while holding the keys to a door opening onto the path to a new life who do not even know the door exists.

As humans, we deny our part in the wrongdoing we choose, deny the acts which put us in the darkness and cost us money, time, love, friendships, relationships, good and healthy environments, peace, and fulfillment. Worse, we will stand and fight against those who come to show us the door and help us find the path to the light beyond.

## EGO AND HOPE

In one word. Our egos tell us not to over share our dark places, not to share our darkest secrets. I read a meme on social media, a clever video with six tips on what to do or not do to gain success, and two of the six tips were never share your secrets and people do not want to know your darkest stories. At the surface both of those statements sound like sage advice. I promise, both are soul depleting. Herein lies the societal push-pull. People who are sheep will follow everything they read or see and will trudge down bad paths. Left to interpretation, many misinterpret good advice because it's wrong when applied to a broken psyche unable to admit truth.

I learned a valuable lesson a couple decades ago. I wrote a harsh email to my subordinates asking them to rise up and march. Those who were already marching the hardest were the first to reply. As if it had been written directly to them, they heard the call to action and swiftly responded in affirmation of the job at hand.

This was as I expected because I could depend on those souls. But the strong message was for the people in the back, the ones who didn't hear the message as loudly and clearly. My hope was to draw them out to fight. Sometimes I was trying to draw those who wanted to fight authority and control to the open space, sometimes they did it loudly, in front of everyone on the email, and I would have to stand and fight like a spectacle, but I was a worthy opponent who used them as an example to others. I was not afraid to convince the defiant man to join a good cause. I stood by my original orders, strong in my belief, and I overcame their objections, convincing them to join the cause. I ultimately won their favor and others followed. This would motivate the mediocre guys.

Still, there would be a group left unshaken. The bottom of the pack, the back of the pack, the ones not listening, not moved or motivated, the disconnected and the deaf. This group who had somehow and at some time joined the cause under false pretenses who coast along on P&Ls as a weight in the boat of great companies taking and hardly giving, those were the folks I wanted to reach most.

I heard long ago a fool's journey in leadership was trying to believe you could get a poor producer, a poor worker to rise to even average levels. Time spent stubbornly trying to prove as leaders you could do this had horrible ROI.

The same time spent with the doers in your group, the top producers, they would give you two times their top production and they were easily motivated for a cause. Knowing this should tell a logical leader where to spend focus. But for me, being as stubborn as I was, I felt there had to be more. There has to be a reason these lost souls are unmotivated, and if I could conjure a fight in even half of them it would be a life-changing gift.

I was willing to put my leadership to the test. Even though logical wisdom told me otherwise, I did invest time in the lower-level producers' success. I discovered in the ranks of the unmotivated and lackadaisical minds of the bottom dwellers many were stuck. They were stuck not knowing how, what, why, when, or where to get on their personal success tracks.

I chose to interview them, ask a ton of business and personal questions. What did they want in life and in wealth? What did they think their targets were and what motivated them or deterred them conversely from reaching those goals? In the answers to these seemingly benign questions lay the symptoms of their illnesses and in all truth, I found many who I could not revive. Over time, I became quicker in making this assessment although never hasty. I was diagnosing the terminally ill.

I found there are fundamental traits for people who do not have the ability to change. In the under-producer realm, the ability to change was either all defeating or lifesaving. Sometimes the words they spoke told me whether they could change. Other times we unlocked a personal plague killing them emotionally and distracting them from a healthy career succession or focus.

Personal lives are never transparent at work and will take down the career of a good man or woman if not addressed. Learning to compartmentalize is vital both to protect yourself and your job. I gave my professionals emotional support by acknowledging their personal strife, suggesting resources, and asking them to set aside their woes while at work. I taught those who were willing to learn the important lesson the most successful people already knew. Everyone has problems at home. Successful people come to work to focus on work and not compound their situation with loss of income or job.

Is it ego to look away from the downtrodden or is it ego to try to raise up those who are capable but lost? I say egotistical managers look away like people walking past the homeless. Their attitude is one of being embarrassed by their employee and not wanting to deal with them.

I personally understand this position. Only some of those on the bottom are salvageable. I am wary of a victim mindset and create healthy boundaries to protect myself from this personality. Sometimes people do die in this area if they can't reset. Others are simply unmotivated at work and have never really been hungry for success. They chose a sales job over punching a clock. They come to work, fly under a proverbial radar, and go through the motions under producing and skating by. These are the true sales parasites we need to identify and extinguish. Sadly, if you took 100 bottom producers, half would be in this category. It's hard to identify them too as they show up as worker bees and don't morph into their real moth-like persona until they have safely passed the protective probation period.

All of this said, I could find the gold in this area more than most people were willing to work to find it. I scoured this area for a given period of time identifying the types of people I had and then lit the fire under the asses of those who I thought I could move. Most of the time I would create a real movement by showing up at their milestones and breakthroughs to continue pouring gasoline on their small yet significant flames. Soon this group became my average and my average sales guys given the same methodology in management would shake out to become some of my top producers.

Every once in a while, I would see life-changing development lead a bottom dweller to become a top producer. This always gave me hope as a leader. These successes, rare as they were, changed my eyesight to value what other leaders considered a waste and led to the resolve I have today of seeing hope in every human being.

Hope and belief are a powerful cocktail for survival and to thrive. This is a cocktail I mix up every day and serve to the masses. Finding the door is a metaphoric philosophy which provides a clear vision for all leaders who encourage others.

If you are the person trying to find the door, I first ask you to look for it. Simple as it may sound, our eyesight when turned towards our sorrow, our grief, or wallowing in the dismay of our lives let downs or hurts, will keep us from finding the door. The strength you need to stand up first and foremost is step one. And if right now standing up seems an impossible task I would ask you to forget about your dreams and hopes, whether short or long term and put all of your focus on the first step because right now your mission is not to conquer the world, it's to take step one, simply put. You need to rest until you can stand and that is all. Your mission then is to stand up. Fight to stand up. And when you can stand up take your first step towards the new door and grab the handle and open it.

It seems so simple to people who want change or need change, but it isn't simple. I have stood before doors a long time before opening them. Finding the door is the mystery the world needs to solve. I am proud to be living in a period of my life where helping people to and from good and bad doors is my full-time job. I guess today I am a doorman and very proud of it.

*CHAPTER 15*

# Escape Artist

Ever have to save yourself from complete demise and not cause a scene while doing it? I have. It's hard work. Not drawing attention to yourself while drowning and flailing around trying to find the shore is an art. To escape your lowest points in life is a task requiring careful calculation. Truly, there is no real way to just disappear and reappear renewed and right all the sudden. There is a true public relations process even in our private lives. We must administer, correct, and heal with watchers gawking. If you can figure out how to do this unscathed you have become a true escape artist while avoiding your own devastation. Everyone will need this skill set in life before they die. Everyone.

I recall the many business scandals I have borne witness to in my career. Anyone reading this who worked with me and knows I witnessed your scandal, don't worry. I'm a vault and will draw upon generalities to reference the points of this chapter.

Many people won't save themselves because the act of doing so draws attention. It is easier to keep silently suffering, silently using, silently being deceitful, or silently dying than to rise and fight.

Fighting means stepping up and out to ask for help. Fighting means coming out of the holes in which we are dying and climbing into the light. And that means facing shit.

Facing shit means getting exposed, affirming your plight, and saying out loud, "I fucked up."

I recall a gentleman who worked with me who got caught in a sex scandal. He was single but was caught with a woman of the evening and the situation included an extortion of his financial assets. While on my watch as an executive leader under our company marquis and brand, I received a weekend phone call from my employee even though he felt insecure and prepared for termination. I carefully considered the first move and asked myself had he committed a crime on work time? The simple answer was no. My advice then to him would be the same now; to cop to what he did fully. He did that.

Instead of defending and justifying his actions leading him down the dark path to walk the plank he was standing on, he walked into Human Resources to find the person who needed to perform protective work on our systems. He admitted all of it in great detail.

As a result, the sentiment of those working with him was an overwhelming feeling of wanting to help him survive his public wrongdoing as best they could, and to move on as quickly as possible from it and thus minimize the loss he would undoubtedly encounter. This is exactly what occurred and as a result, he became an escape artist of this situation. He stood, dealt, and then was met with swift clean up. His losses were harsh as family and friends had seen the social media repair that was unavoidable since he was exposed on social media by a hacker who had posted pornographic level photos of him and this lady who was part of a scheme to extort him. Aunts and nieces, colleagues and friends all saw this situation unfold in real-time.

Because he swiftly acted to inform us as his employer, we were able to address issues, and helped him navigate the extortion part. In the end, he avoided any monetary losses from the extortionist, willing to accept their threats and actions and not overpay these thieves to avoid it.

What would you have done? It is a question I asked myself when he told me. Then, I feel I would have paid any amount of money to avoid public humiliation. I was in awe of the process and choices made by this individual to move to the other side. I was empathetic to his plight, and I also knew this low moment would not define him in the end. We do not need to remain stuck in our lowest mistake. And giving someone permission to forgive themselves is a gift beyond measure.

Another time I received a middle-of-the-night call for a legal situation where cops had been called to a hotel by a husband who had caught his wife at said motel with our manager. Same process as above occurred. Job was saved, mess cleaned up, the parties escaped public demise by swift and transparent action. For a few days the entire situation was dire and the level of gravity intense. Interesting for me in this situation was watching the fallout of loyalty. Trust me, people choose sides when the fire blazes. They will run out of your burning building fast. When the heat turns up people want no part of it. If you are fortunate to find those who will stand in the heat with you, consider these forever friends. Be wary of those who run and take note, they will circle back a lot of times after the dust settles with some excuse and reason they left. Don't believe them. They made a choice, and their choice was to let you sit in your own crap. We have choices on both sides of the blaze in life, to stand in and with or run and high tail it out of a bad situation. We must make good choices on both sides.

For me, my loyalty is unbreakable. Ask anyone who has served with me to bear witness. I have stood in honor through countless situations and been unshakeable. My barometer is always honesty and goodness. Even when I was not at my most honest my autopilot would steer me towards being loyal to good people. Had these people messed up? Yes. Was their building on fire? Yes. Was I pissed at times they had made bad choices? Yes. Did I run? No. I never ran. I never will. I am a mighty fire-fighter.

I had to clean up my world many times for similar situations. I once had an affair with someone, I hate to say, and in my realization of guilt and a desire to end it, I had to come clean and move past it. In the end my relationship didn't survive this, but my inner integrity was preserved. This is the point I am trying to make. I could sit here since this is my own story and add the reasons. I felt lonely and compelled to allow myself to let another person in for example, but I won't. I won't justify the wrongdoing here or anywhere else. I operated during those days with tremendous guilt and shame, even though the entire time I was justifying this in my own head.

Another time I needed to admit myself for a detox due to a prescription painkiller addiction I had found myself in following a car accident. I could not get off them without getting sick, and the truth was I was abusing them. I would go through more than was prescribed and had found underground outlets to supply myself between prescriptions. In theory, I was a drug addict and performing illegal actions. Sounds dramatic, but it happens every day. I tried drying out during a vacation and couldn't without getting violently sick; the only way through this was to tell my family and friends and head on in to rehab, which I did at an in-facility rehab center.

Doing this was not minor.

There was no escaping. The only way through this situation was transparency and total admission I needed help. I recall the look on my parents' faces as I shared my need to enter rehab: shock and utter dismay. I was an accomplished professional when this occurred. I know it was disappointing and alarming for them and for all who knew me.

When I flew to the rehab facility, I was very sick. My pancreas was failing, and I had many physical ailments brought on by the drug abuse. I wasn't sleeping well or consistently, my diet, eating habits, and even bathroom habits were all compromised. Again, here is the complete truth serum of this story: I was sick as a dog and killing myself slowly and methodically. The human body is not intended to endure anything of a non-holistic nature, and I was polluting myself at a deep level daily.

I had always been warned self-medicating was a killer of extraordinary levels. I carried major guilt and hurt for not helping solve the end of my marriage to my son's father, and I had broken vows to God, which for me was extremely serious. I remember the pills taking the edge off the heartache I carried daily.

Heartache compromised everything else in my life. Walking around with a broken heart and with guilt changes your reaction to the world. It changes how fast you react to hard situations, and how hard you react to them. When just below the surface of your world lays enormous pain, you will flail your arms in defense without proper regard to the gravity of the situation.

I woke with hurt, I lived with hurt, I lay with hurt every day. Then one day I cracked my C-7 vertebrae in my neck due to a car accident. Pile on physical hurt on top of a broken heart, and I was a proverbial mess.

Then the most wonderous and backhanded gift was offered, I was given these little pills to help with the pain. Guess what? The pills dulled the aching depths of the ongoing emotional pain I suffered.

Suddenly, I was able to work and think, laugh again and not dwell. That was a gift I recall of enormous proportions. I remember being so grateful for the relief. I slept, ate, and played again. My past haunts were a fading memory finally, and I was able to move on to heal my broken heart. But, as with all things, too much is too much and sometimes too much is a death threat.

I have studied about the addictive levels of opiates and discovered 18 out of 20 people (ten being of a genetic background prone to addiction) become addicted to this drug. Physically the break down occurs when your brain is getting blocker signals from pain, emotional or physical. The side effects when you do not take it are increasing levels of pain, shaking hands and quivering, sweating as your body goes into detox, doubling over with stomach cramps, headaches, and overall excruciating body pain.

I tried to dry out when I realized I had an issue. Each time I tried I awakened in a bed of sweat and pain, wobbling to the sink in the bathroom, hands shaking, looking at myself in the mirror, I downed my first dose before even brushing my teeth and was quickly restored to a base level of functioning, one which leveled me up to where I needed to be to get through my morning routine.

With the pain pills, I operated fully working and managing this daily routine, but it became a job. Every day and week I needed to ensure I was medicinally covered; I would count pills to ensure I could get from one end to the other of my life. It was a new chain and ball replacing the old chain and ball. Now I had a new problem, and even worse, the old problem hadn't really been dealt with. The pain hadn't disappeared; it was all still there under the surface, and it was masked.

I knew to go forward I had to stop the new problem and deal with the old problem before restoring myself to true health.

This part of my journey to the integrity and healing I desired was like climbing an impossible mountain. I stood at the base of looking up and thinking there was no way I would survive the climb. I found myself at the base camp of this journey believing I would die on the mountain.

When the admission personnel of the rehab center frisked me and stripped me of my belongings, clothes and, cell phone, I was vividly aware of my plight. Escorted out of the security room with a prayer card and a picture of my son, I made my way to my room. I was only hours into my detox, having been instructed to stay high until I got there and to bring all remaining drugs. My supply had dwindled and I had not much left when I came in. I recall in the days after I was admitted seeing how absolutely intoxicated everyone arrived at the center because they went go on Hail Mary binges before walking in, which might be counter-intuitive as it prolonged the front-end recovery process, but still it was common.

I remember the flagrant personalities of the inebriated in their initial days, me too, no doubt. Even though I was frustrated with where I was, I recall thinking I was happy to be at a place where I could answer to the first big leg of my journey to complete rehabilitation. I wanted it. I was ready. I had self-admitted without any intervention or fanfare. I was there of my own admission which made me self-accountable. I surrendered to the depths of addiction and said, "I need help."

The people who walked with me from the base camp of this climb were truly remarkable. The first person who took me from admissions was this tall bald white guy. He was wearing a sleeveless shirt and I recall he had bullets on his arms with dates next to them. I thought it was a memorial to loved ones; I later learned those represented people he supposedly killed. He had been a member of the Colombian drug cartel. The facility was in Florida and as such this made some sense to me. He was missing an eye and not wearing a patch (true story). He was kind and not scary to me despite his appearance. He was, after all, someone escorting me into a hospital. I was about to join the likes of him for many more days and weeks.

On the long walk to my room, I recall thinking I was nothing like the people I saw lining the hallways in pajama-like clothing, all looking as if they'd had better days. I soon would come to terms with the reality I was one of them. I was. I was no different. I mean, we were all different in ethic and economic ways, but we were just the same.

I was a rough case for the rehab facility. We discovered on day two an allergy to the detox drug caused me to get so sick on top of the detox process, and I was taken from the facility by ambulance to the local hospital. I remained there unconscious for days on IV and was not even aware I had left the facility.

I believe it was day five when I returned to the rehab facility. I had piqued the curiosity of my hospital mates; I am sure they asked themselves what had I done to be so sick the rehab center was not equipped to handle my detox? I recall laying in the bunk in the room I shared with a woman from Virginia. She was recovering from a combination of alcohol and drug addictions. I returned from the hospital incredibly sick still, and I lie in the bed unable to move for another two days.

During that time, an elderly lady came to sit with me and read from a book I bought at the airport on the way there. The book, titled Little Bee, was about a Nigerian girl who escaped as a refugee to England after watching her entire family slain and told the story of her survival in that detention center. I remember listening intently with my eyes closed to the voice of this woman I didn't know. She was simply a wonderful human who came to sit with me in my sickness out of the pureness of her heart or the sorrow of her empathy towards my plight. On day seven, she brought me chicken broth in a Styrofoam cup with saltines and encouraged me to eat. I recall not wanting to eat, but she left it on my shelf and later I sipped the soup and ate one saltine. I slept for long periods on those days.

On day eight, I was required to join the group session. I understood this was an Alcoholics Anonymous program and all rehabbers had to go to group, whether or not you were there for alcohol addiction. I somehow made my way to the community room, across the court by way of a path wearing only a light robe with wet hair fresh from the shower I finally took for the first time in a week.

I was not this big stand out when I entered the room filled with 50 sick people. Each person was in some state of recovery. I made my way to the back of the room and prayed I would not be called on to speak. The men and women in the room stared at me as I watched people share intimate stories of both sadness and victory. I could not hide and was asked to say my name. For the first time in a week, I spoke, saying simply, "Christine," and everyone replied, "Hello Christine." Thus was my official anointment in a club no person ever wants to join. I knew the moment I spoke my name; anonymity was forever dissolved.

In the days after I was taken to an oncology center near the hospital for a full cat scan examination of my pancreas and liver. The oncology center was in an elite area of Florida, and I was accompanied by a facility worker and transported by van. I became agitated while waiting for this process, the facility worker sat with me in the waiting room, and I was obviously being surveyed by the other patients, many of whom appeared to be in full cancer treatment and looked at me as I sat with this big, black female hospital guard. I was highly irritated with this situation as I walked out of the hospital. Suddenly, before I knew what was happening, I was running away from the hospital. I remember thinking I could lose this guard by running even though I didn't know where I was going. I just wanted to prove I was stronger than her.

What is incredible to me to realize in hindsight is how sick I had been and how my anger fueled me to push my broken body down this street at a high speed. I looked back and I could see her talking into her walkie-talkie thingy and heard her say, "Patient has escaped." I thought to myself, "Am I running right now?" And suddenly I stopped and sat hard on the street curb.

I recall how beautiful an area I was in; palm trees abounding in a clearly wealthy area, and here I was, a rehab patient running from a guard. I thought to myself, "Is this really happening right now?" Sure enough, as if pinching my way out of a dream, it became clear this was my real life and this WAS happening to me.

I heard the pounding of big feet on the sidewalk behind me and the words, "Get up," and so I did. As I turned, she said, "I have called for backup."

I said, "Why? Are you hurt?" I walked briskly by her side down the street and back on foot to the cancer hospital. I returned to the waiting room, but she did not come in. She was sweating and breathing hard for an additional 20 minutes and stayed outside. I was pretty sure she was calling family members because as the door to the hospital opened and closed, I could pick up pieces of her rant, "...and then she ran, and I couldn't catch her." I remember thinking, "That's right bitch you couldn't catch me."

I don't know why I felt the need to run and yet, for the first time in years, I felt alive again. I felt angry and emotional and not dulled and depressed. I recognized the return of my vigor at that moment, and I suddenly realized I was going to feel again. I welcomed the feelings I had wished away long ago. I remember feeling nostalgic as if I had been away on a vacation from my own emotions.

The next thing I heard was my name being called to be seen for my cat scan. Christine Beckwith.

For the first time in eight days, I was no longer anonymous in a protective center. I realized in a startling moment what a really bad place I was in, a place where truly sick people existed, and not because they put that illness upon themselves, but because out of bad luck, they were dying from an illness and fighting it.

Only the fight was common between us. I was fighting, too. I realized I didn't believe I deserved to be cancer free. This place was about to tell me the damages the doctor had seen in my liver and pancreas. I was told a few days later I had non-cancerous liver lesions and pancreatitis, both common afflictions from drug addiction. I was now permanently damaged from this abuse. I could recover from the pancreatitis, but my liver would forever be scarred. Even though I still didn't feel I deserved to be cancer free, I recognized God had given me a new lease on life.

I was fighting to escape the unbearably strong hold of addiction and I was winning. I realized a truth I live to this day; I need to conquer today. This thought has been the same for me for ten years now, and I know every day I wake up I choose to appreciate this gift of time.

As for the hospital guard, she reported me, and I faced a principal's office visit, per se. I spent my 20 minutes giving a business review of her demeanor, from the personal calls she made to her behavior to, during, and from the hospital, until the conversation was no longer about me being scolded for running but about whether a guard should be able to be outsmarted by an angry patient. I escaped penalty. She was not my fan for the remainder of the visit, which came with some trepidation on my part as I was, in fact, being detained in the facility. Self-admitted yes but living in a locked-down environment in which at any time the guard could enter my room. But that did not happen, and every day I became more and more clear and more and more alive.

I counted the minutes until I could return to my family, my son, and my boyfriend, and I knew when I did, I would be a different person from the zombie who had left weeks prior. I knew I needed them to see I could save myself. I knew also I needed to come out ready to address the deeper issues I had suppressed for many years prior, the issues leading me to the mysterious moment where a strong, successful woman could take a tiny pill for a neck injury and be pulled into the devil's web. It happens every single day to normal humans all across the world. Fix one problem and make another. I am fully aware now, and today and forever since I fought this battle, my eyesight is trained on ensuring I never accidentally slide down the slippery slope of addiction again.

I want to be clear on something else. I didn't have a garden variety addiction. I was taking dosages of painkillers. It happened gradually, after years of my prescription being increased and added upon by other narcotic prescriptions building to a dosage capable of killing a large man.

The thing about pain killers is you become immune to their power and slowly you increase the dosage until one day the amount is so staggering if you suddenly stop you might die of the side effects of the detox without medical attention. I do not wish anyone I love or even hate to travel down this road.

I consider myself to be an intelligent person. Addiction happened without my logical or conscious awareness. When I was ready to stop taking the painkillers, even advocating for myself with my physicians for help would prove to be a dead-end street because they are not equipped to support the rehabilitation process. They can write the prescriptions and they can make it harder and harder to get them, but the sad truth is, it's not hard to get sick in America. An even sadder truth is, it's far harder to get well. The work I had to perform to be approved by health care and then find a bed took days and weeks of concerted effort and happened only because I truly wanted to make this happen.

To say this was the lowest point of my life would be a huge understatement. I know many people would never admit this to others. I have contemplated my ability to write this chapter while standing in truth. I realized truth is part of my journey and writing this book is part of truth. The story of each path I walked to get to where I am today must be shared. The lessons we can learn through these situations are greatest for those who need to know you can conquer your mountains too. That is truly the message here.

I remained in the rehab facility, attending both group and individual sessions for rehabilitation. I remember those who were with me. At least three out of 52 who were part of my group, sadly, died of their illnesses. One died only days after I left the facility. He was a father of two small children fighting alcoholism. Although we were sworn to never speak of the things shared in group, in private I remember him telling a story about his young daughter giving him monopoly money saying she would help pay for things. He broke down as he spoke the words out loud, recognizing his young daughter's fear their home was not safe or secure. He knew he was failing her as a father.

I have often thought how incredible it would be to find his daughter one day and share those words from her deceased father. Would it matter for her to know how sad inside her father was with his illness and how much he recognized his need to fight for his integrity?

What has stood out for me these many years is all of those wretched souls fighting for their honesty. Fighting a battle to get off a road they sadly found themselves on for a million reasons. Lost souls trying to find their way. I learned many of them were repeat offenders. They had been in rehab many times, some of them, and still they fought. Sometimes we have to fight a battle more than once to win it and sometimes we die trying. Glory is found in the fight and in our desire to win life's battles.

I won my battle and prevailed. I reached the mountain top and I've not turned back on the other side of the climb. I am keenly aware of the power of drugs.

I went to work immediately following my sobriety battle to heal my mental wellness. This work was deeper than anything I have ever done. I went down a rabbit hole with my counselor twice a month for ten years all the way back to my mother's childhood and my own, and to reason with maternal strife I felt, to reason with abandonment issues I lived with, to reason with trust issues I carry, to forgive myself for my contributions to destroying a sacred part of my child's life, his family, and the hope he had for a normal biological family setting.

I had punished myself long enough. I had pushed myself to the brink of survival trying to destroy my guilt. I came up gasping for air only when I had nearly killed myself and realizing I would die if I didn't change course.

To do work of that magnitude, to sit with my mother's childhood upbringing the best I knew it, piecing together with facts I carried from elders who shared and my own memory, I came to understand how I had become who I was and who raised me and why they were like they were and more. In the end a picture emerged of a damaged person who had to unlearn bad traits which were suffocating my relationships.

I know now I ran from healthy love to chase an attention-filling-bottomless need for love. I was lacking in self-value based on a subconscious belief I had from my childhood. I compare finding this truth to searching for impossibly lost treasure. If you can go on the journey to find it, you have everything. The journey itself will bear fruit as fighting is a powerful confidence booster. I was willing to fight and make the long trek. Whether I would reach the other side was something only I could know by doing it. I believed I would.

And I did. I saved myself in the end. I did the work I had not, for many years, been able to do. I am still now saving myself every day. I have come to realize we will perpetually be saving ourselves and renewing. This fight never really has an ending while we are alive and living. We must become wiser and stronger in our ability to fight and be self-honest. We must come to terms with this need to fight for who we are being an ever constant in our lives until we die.

There is no age limit on fighting this fight. I remember events near the end of my great-grandmother and my great aunts' lives which showed they reached out, learned, and grew in their final years. For those of us who remain curious and desire evolution, we will never tire of learning nor stop wanting to know more, about this incredible world. We will always want to work on ourselves.

# CHAPTER 16

# Standing Down

During the first 20 years of my career, I was corralled into political correctness. Born from a strong and stern mother who has a sharp tongue, my lessons learned by observation and example were to strike and let the dust settle. I watched this continually for the first 18 years of my life. My mother didn't hold back. Many times, it was in public and embarrassing to me, and I really disliked it.

In later years, I grew to admire her ability to be outspoken. I know amongst her peers at the factory where she worked when my sisters and I were growing up, she often spoke for her coworkers. I never knew how hard it was for people to speak up and say how they truly felt. I was lucky not to have to suppress my feelings. As a result, I was a free spirit to the nth degree.

As a child, speaking was an issue for me when I felt unable to share equal time with my classmates. I had my hand in the air for every question. I loved to talk. My kindergarten report card says so, "Christine can't stop talking." I remember wondering to myself if this was a bad thing. Ha, ha!

Today as a professional speaker, I am still talking and I have not run out of stuff to say, not even close. As a child I had teachers who saw it both as a strength and a detriment. For those who saw my speaking as a strength, I would be given a voice, an opportunity to share my words. Some helped me write. I published poems and writings as a child as my skills in writing and speaking were being honed. As a young grade schooler, I sought my first democratic role as a student council president. I won it with my ability to rally support through spoken words and leadership.

Continuing into high school, I served many leadership roles and took extra English classes as well and served as a tutor in English. I wrote for the school newspaper, and I took public speaking classes. I found myself in front of the microphone in high school and I enjoyed sharing words. I had a fear of public speaking but found joy in inspiring others through words, which I could see I had power in doing.

It was not until I reached corporate America I was met with many men trying to shut me up and stop me from speaking. I find humor in this statement, but it's quite literally true. I was an over communicator and I have accepted today that is who I am. I have found the way to communicate and benefit others with books, curriculum, guidance, and motivation.

For several adult decades I was asked to stand down on topics, projects, or sentiments the politically correct world of corporate America didn't pray to. I never understood why companies wanted polished opinions, other than to control the dialogue. I can tell you I died a slow death daily in that environment and I found my way being who I was in that world.

I didn't really fit in. I won't lie. I hate to admit it because I had all the ingredients of a good leader, but the truth is I was too outspoken to avoid ruffling feathers. It was impossible truly to avoid. I didn't realize this until long after I left. While I was there, I thought I could stay in line and my inner voice had lots of conversations about staying in line.

I didn't want to be a standout person. I didn't want to feel like I often did. I noticed if you had me in an eight-hour all-day meeting, somewhere around the five-to-six hour mark I was going to verbally assault someone and I laugh saying that. I could only sit and wait my turn for so long in a room where speaking meant being quiet for long periods of time.

I learned to wait my turn. As a long-time interrupter, I am still recovering today and work on it continuously. Raised by an interrupter from a long line of interrupters, I am recovering.

Sitting quietly was not my jam, let's say. I didn't do well with it. I found myself much more at ease in front of the room, even being the person who emceed the meeting I would have an active role in the conversation throughout. I am sure people saw that as attention seeking and maybe it was, the jury is still out as to my motivation for attention. Perhaps motivation is too strong a word choice here; I had a nearly unquenchable thirst for attention.

I love to be heard. I love to move people with words. I could be talking about how to wash yourself and I would have a start, middle, and strong finish on the subject. I think I could have been a great defense attorney or prosecutor. I am certain

I could slay with words. I never was on my high school debate team, but I could dismantle a person with words because I would remember everything you ever said to me and if you lied in any way, shape, or form, or if you varied from the previous story, my trust in you would diminish and with it my faith you were a whole person.

And since so few whole people work in corporate America, I was often amid a bunch of totally unemotional people who I truly believe were not like me, by and large. I felt like I suffered most of my adult life within this environment, despite winning sales contests and rising rapidly through the ranks of my peers to hold senior level sales roles for three decades.

I love competing. I love inspiring people to compete. I love the feeling of a hard-fought victory. I learned skills by reading and meeting Tim Grover, who wrote the NY Times Best Selling books, *Winning* and *Relentless*. He calls people who will go through hell and back to reach goals *cleaners*. That's me. And that is the part I love. Standing down was not my jam.

In fact, I now understand the neglect I felt from most of my bosses was actually not feeling heard. If you didn't react how I wanted, you were enemy #1 for me and in the politically correct world of corporate America I was as much wildly disregarded as I was leaned upon to finish the job. I was brought in for the hard jobs, given the clerical work, the difficult mathematics, the under-dog teams, the ultimate goal chaser projects, the reworks and the redoes, and I was trusted fully to complete the job. I was not really respected by my managers because they all thought I was coming for their job. I had a way of making the guy in front of me feel nervous and I consistently did my whole career.

The guys working for me knew my steely ways. They would stand and fight with me for the cause and I would muster the words to make their buy-in formidable. I still feel I can do the same today.

Standing down for me was a completely sickening feeling, a corporate illness many are suffering with right now. Standing up, on the other hand, was my jam. I loved a good debate, a good defense, a good sell, or a good proving of something regarded as impossible.

Standing up meant standing alone. Standing up meant having a real relationship with right or wrong while being aware which side of the fence you stood on, in every way.

We can't stand up when we are standing down. We can't be warriors in life for others when we stand down. We can't change the hardships of our own life or others if we stand down. We can't be free if we stand down. The list of losses and potential deficits brought on by standing down is huge and frightens many from standing up.

I stood down for a long time. I turned a blind eye to unsavory things; I did unsavory things in my day. It was easier to go along to get along. The roads of doing bad are riddled with people while the paths to honesty are desolate and lonely. To move from one to the other, you must be willing to stand apart and stay strong. Be convicted in your word and you become almighty powerful in your journey.

I had false power. I thought money, prestige, titles, and awards made me powerful. I am decorated in this life which proves I am a worthy soldier but the worth of leadership cannot be given. The worth of a following cannot be bought. Those who don't see you will stray. True fellowship comes from showing yourself nakedly, exposing your demerits, letting the world view your scarred and broken truths, and having people stay with you anyway. When a man remains at your table when there is no food you know you have a friend.

In the end, learning who I was, how I was wired and standing up meant changing lives and doing greater work. In the most meaningful way, my inner belief in how I can move the needle in people's lives is how I eventually fell back in love with myself. The day I looked in the mirror and liked what I saw was decades apart from the last time I felt that way. I had been lured away by deceit and humanly physical attractions. Left broken and unwilling to fight for myself, I trudged for years following a realm of self-serving and not soul supporting rules imposed by society.

The day I decided to start coloring outside the lines again, I took my life back. I began to spread my wings. I have never looked back, and I never will. I know the dead ends now and I know what to do and not to do.

I am no longer able to keep my words inside me and I am no longer able to lie. I catch myself embellishing things and adjust all the time. When I say my calibration for truth is almighty it is kind of shocking to even me as I kind of liked being a bad ass. Now I am a bad ass human truth teller, and there is fun in that and honor. I am finding my honor and I continue to gain ground every day.

*CHAPTER 17*

# Newfound Eyesight

I am sitting in my home office and living now in the pandemic years, something I never thought of in a million years could occur in modern times. We are currently in social distancing mode. The second phase from a global lock down brought on by the COVID-19 pandemic spread that has killed thousands of people this year. Our only safe means of interaction with other humans currently is video messaging through phone or laptop.

I am just coming off a two-hour video call with Jay Doran. How our lives have transformed. The years we spent meeting at Flemings for late night philosophical dinners in New Jersey have given way to coffee dates over video. In fact, we were officially in session, as he remains my coach. I continue doing

deep philosophical and business dives with Jay, who is guiding me beyond personal development. I have listened, and I have learned, I have applied, and I have grown with his incredibly intelligent and uber sense of human behaviors.

I have also been the benefactor of thousands upon thousands of hours of his own self-teaching, reading the great philosophers and studying them, and applying their methodologies. I have given myself to someone who I trust ultimately and unconditionally, and who has proven to be trustworthy. The faith I put in Jay long ago when others pointed at him, mocked him, called him a weirdo, and who measured him by a blank slate of success he didn't yet possess, has never wavered. I chose to measure him by his worth and integrity as I saw it; no material matter was part of the equation.

It's funny because the person who was loudest about the lack of value Jay brought to the table was a person who lacked character and self-integrity, who was lost in the world. This person's measuring stick for human value was broken, his eyesight to judge human worth was marred. It was an easy decision not to fall victim to his pressure. His pressure at times was loud as he shared his opinion with many others. I chose to ignore it, not out of rebellion, which was how it was seen at the time but rather out of an understanding he who judged was to be judged himself one day. And because of a pure and real belief in Jay who, while meeting the definition of a person lacking in worldly value at that time, was rich in the most beautiful of ways.

Today Jay is one of the most sought-after coaches and consultants in my industry and mainstream America. His clientele are the extremely successful, richest humans on earth. Now seen by all as a person with value, his gifts have been unearthed and acknowledged, his beauty understood and exposed. I am no less committed to him than I was so many years ago when, under pressure to not talk to him, leveled by my peers at the office who thought he was nuts, I persevered. If he was nuts, then so was I. We were two crazy, egotistical, social media-crazed people relegated as losers. How wrong could someone be?

Why was the judgement all damning for Jay and me? Because we chose to keep our eyes trained on what we believed in our hearts was the right direction. Together we forged forward and walked the path together being real with one another. We exposed each other's deficits. We pointed out dangers in our peripheral.

I don't want to paint this incorrectly; we were not equal in this relationship, not in the slightest, although I know Jay would tell you he has learned so much from me as I shared everything I know about growing a business to help him grow his own business. I was 100 percent Jay's student. He the teacher and me the person looking for guidance.

I submitted myself to Jay as if God had sent him to me because that is my belief, as the opening of this book states. I still believe he is a godly presence in my life. I believe God tested my faith in bringing Jay to me, asking me if I had strong enough faith to put all of it into the human Jay was back then, lacking worldly riches and chastised by naysayers. Could I see his value and believe? God knows I did and do.

On this morning Jay and I dove into facing my ego. I dismantled actions driven by a desire to fill an attention-seeking need. On this day, I came to terms with why I wasn't fully accepted for my gifts. This understanding had eluded me for many years. I knew in my heart I was good, but because I was filling a bottomless void of love for myself, I drove from a good place with the wrong thirst. I hadn't always done things for the right reasons. I hadn't always been a man of the people. I had often wanted the trophy as if that would finally magically make me believe I was good. The truth was I had an internal belief I was not good, and I had spent a lifetime trying to prove I was. Jay helped me see this break in myself and this is when the real work began, work which would change me forever.

I don't mind admitting I disliked Jay greatly during this process. I never stopped internally loving him, but I was angry with him, and I fought him with words. Often when he would ask me a question, I would rise and defend myself. I also think he listened, and through those moments of conflict, he learned I was not someone driven by material things.

Ironically, giving way to the insatiable appetite for wrongful attention, I began driving from this place with great GPS for the right reasons and the riches came so much easier. I was rewarded again, as if from God, even in one of the hardest of my times in my business life. I was on my own starting from ground zero, having left the place I thought would bring me the most riches, serving an industry tirelessly but in an ungodly way and boom, the flood-gates aligned and opened.

It's unmistakable to me now in hindsight. Jay is my Sherpa, carefully and confidently reassuring me when I weary of my next step.

He and I are way down a Godly taken road. We are both healthier than we ever have been. Our circles are tight and our friendships strong. We have secured our families with greater incomes and are working with our gifts daily, now aligned fully.

The path to get here was not easy for either one of us. The depths of our friendship now expands to our families and business circles. I am in love with his better half, if you will, Jenna. She has brought incredible value to the table for me, both in business relations and friendship. She is an incredible complement to Jay's brilliance with brilliance of her own. Together, they are an almighty force in the world known by their company name Culture Matters. My family has benefited from knowing both of them. My son has been given books and guided through deep philosophical discussions one-on-one and in groups by Jay. We have had family meetings where we resolved family issues and communication styles, as hoaky as it sounds. The boys have sat in the think tank which is Jay and Jenna's hot tub in their Florida home, until pruned, talking into the depths of philosophy. We are all better for it.

My eyesight is sharp now. I think of these song lyrics, "I can see clearly now the rain is gone," and yet I know there will be more rain to come, and even greater storms ahead. As an extreme empath, I will not escape the pain of loss in my future, and I will have to survive the depths of despair. I will need to lead my company through rough markets, stand in conflict, and face and embrace the uncomfortableness of it. I will do good work because of my ability to do so.

Today, because of the techniques I have self-administered with Jay's guidance I am able to keenly guide others. Drawing upon a pattern of understanding my own growth and turning those into lessons, I am able to give better eyesight to others as well.

I think the biggest change I can point to is what we look at and where we drive to naturally are not always the best or most nourishing places for our lives. We must apply emotional and intellectual intelligence and not a go-with-it mentality. Our natural inclinations are sinful. Our physical drives are often sinful as well.

We must navigate the waters of our life with incredible applied intelligence and discipline. We must be accountable for our actions, and realize we can't just wing it in life. We must do hard things to align ourselves.

Can we ever put our lives on autopilot? I think we can intermittently, but I think that comes from first stepping onto the right road. Are you on the right road? Are you surrounded by the right people?

Have you ever thrown anyone out of your boat wrongfully? Did you choose to stop loving someone or be loved and guided by someone you believed in because of the pressure of some other force? If so, this may be the moment you've been waiting for to circle back and fix those broken relationships.

Being given the eyesight will have a keener sense of accuracy for you when you surround yourself with those who are here to help you rise up. Think about your circle. There are probably people from whom you can create healthy boundaries and people who you can let back in. Or even let go of.

Newfound eyesight for me today, many years now down the road is something I protect with great force. I know everyday decisions could take me off this path. I am mindful to protect where I am sitting. I am careful who to let sit at my table. I will let the people who don't like my integrity walk away, even when painful, because they simply aren't aligned.

Yes, today I can see and again I thank God for bringing Jay to me and guiding me to this newfound eyesight. I will protect it with my life and for the rest of my life. What a gift it is. I will not squander it.

An early photo of Jay and Christine, circa 2017. In this photo Jay visits Christine in Philadelphia where she was lecturing about her then best-selling book, *Clear Boundaries*.

Jay in my red chair in the den of my Pelham, NH home. One of many in-depth professional and personal development sessions.

## AN UNEXPECTED BLESSING: LES BROWN AND JAY

*An Editorial Note:*

The writing of the foreword to this book by Les Brown came about during the hiring of him to speak at one of the 20/20 Vision Summits. Brokered by Culture Matters, Jay had the opportunity to sit with Les and share Christine's story as part of the preparation for Les Brown's speech. In doing so, Les Brown became so moved by her story he stood on stage and surprisingly announced his gift to her in the promise to write her foreword.

It should not be lost on the readers how this incredible gift would have never occurred had it not been for Christine putting her faith in Jay when many others could not see his light.

The very essence of the message in *Finding Honor*, of placing hope and belief in others, is played out in the making of this book in real form and life. The act of professional development as the means to the power and purpose of your life is also clearly ever present in the writing of Jay and Christine's story.

# CHAPTER 18

# The Pain Point

Unbelievable, excruciating pain. Ever feel it? I try to recall when my relationship with emotional and physical pain first proved to be debilitating to me; I think it was when I had my first little romantic break-up as a budding adolescent. I remember lying in bed feeling absolutely devastated. I recall feeling physically sick. I became sick. That repeated itself over my teenage years, and I remember feeling as though nobody's words were able to reason with me or offer soothing; nobody understood my depths of despair.

I remember thinking about killing myself at 18 and knowing this kind of unwanted thought was not normal. Was I abnormal? I wondered. I learned later with counseling about the truly deep emotional barometer I possess. To be clear, my emotional barometer was not broken. I felt the right feelings in the correct settings. When I hurt, I felt sad; when I was happy, I felt joyous, and so on.

However, the height of my happiness and sadness knew no limits. I seem to have no ceiling or floor for either one and without protective boundaries or the knowledge of this, I have come to learn to operate within with self-discipline. I rose to perilous heights and fell to devastating depths. I first learned about this in my early twenties when in the incredible grip of depression. My battle with pain and learning and unlearning began then.

I navigate life as a high feeler (which is known by many other stigmatic labels). It has been a life-long journey to understand what it means to be a high feeler. After two admissions for depression and many years beyond continuing to learn, I understand I have no control over being a high feeler. What I had to learn is to live in the safest environment I can create. By safe, I mean avoid being in trigger situations, protect my psyche, and exercise extreme discipline to feed the positive side of my emotional balance. I tip the scales to the manic side today which is my safe zone.

What is your relationship with pain? Of course, even the most ordinary people suffer pain. It's not like some of us feel and some don't. It's about people adapting every day to deal with what is occurring for them mentally.

I am proud of the world I have created now in my life, where I have helped in many mindset areas, which is a complete outlier by most people's measurements of tactical business coaching. I happen to believe it's a precursor to success.

We are the drivers of our race cars. Our race cars are our businesses. But we must be physically ready to race the car. Do you know how much brute strength it takes to race a car?

Many of us get in the car when we're not strong enough to race. We can putter along, and keep the car going, but we are in no way ready to race our businesses. And yet, we must.

Life is a racetrack, whether we like it or not. We can sit on the sidelines or bring our car into the pit for repair, but we must go back out and race. I want to dedicate this chapter that might otherwise seem dark to learning about pain and some deep-dive tips on self-sustaining methods for betterment and moving out of pain. If you are reading this book right now and suffering, you are NOT alone. I am here, right now, with you.

After my first marriage ended in divorce, I experienced great depression. In addition, I lost my family cat, Harley, to a devastating accident. He ran, frightened, from my apartment in a snowstorm when a mailman dropped a package (a package that was not mine BTW) and jumped a fence into a dog pen, where he was mauled and lost his life. At the time, Harley was all I had in life. I talked to him as if he was a human. I swear, he was consoling me. Harley would lay with me at night and love on me when I cried myself to sleep.

## THE PATH OUT OF PAIN

I recall about this time a counselor gave me a book which was transitional for me. As I read the words of people who were going through what I was, I felt less alone. I hope in this book, *Finding Honor*, others who are searching will find help and perhaps their own transitional experience.

Here are questions and possible answers to consider your relationship and path out of pain.

- On a scale of 1-10, where is your emotional pain? Consider 10 to be the worst strife you have ever experienced, and zero being you're happy and not in any extra emotional pain; zero being the base level.

- Measuring the depths of your pain will allow you to start from a place of knowing the gravity in which you're coping, and counteractions are adequately prescribed.

  *0-5 scale is a normal range of pain although still living with it.*

  *Do you feel like you are managing it OK?*

  *Do you have bouts of emotions but can walk away from the feeling of sadness and into what brings you happiness?*

- 6-10 is a high range and living with this unbearable pain is hard.

  *Do you feel like you are dying inside?*

  *Are you unable to function?*

  *Do you have debilitating pain?*

How deeply you experience pain can be the precursor to understanding you can't change this relationship. You will never change your relationship with pain until you understand how powerful you feel. And as a high feeler I have come to terms with the fact that I am gifted in this way, but it is a double-edged sword and I can ultimately experience love, joy, and happiness at levels of a superior form.

Some of the most painful places in my life showed up to deter me at work, and I had to learn vast coping mechanisms. I can look back now and realize how unequipped I was when I lived in the corporate America environment. I am, at my core, essentially non-compliant. That said, I led the compliance charge as a senior sales leader which eventually meant falling into the politically correct line I was expected to live in and help others do the same. Events would happen at work and internally floor me. In the public eye, I had to choose to hide it or ride it like a bucking bull until I could deal with it.

By the way, I fooled no one. Everyone knew what I was feeling or thinking most of the time. Because I started in the mortgage industry as a young adult, I literally grew up within it. With age and experience came maturity and I eventually became better at keeping my own counsel. The higher I rose in the executive levels, the higher the stakes rose for me to ensure I showed up with sound, objective thinking.

I developed a muscle for compartmentalizing pain. I can still do this today; however, the cat is entirely out of the bag now.

I laugh out loud writing this. Anyone who now knows me knows I speak my mind freely these days, and sadly, I would probably never be able to fit back into that world again. As an example, when I first became the VP of Sales at H&R Block Mortgage.

I won the seat in a stiff competition after a decade of service. Of course, I didn't know the mortgage industry was heading for the iceberg, and we were all unknowing passengers on the Titanic at the time. If I had a crystal ball, I might have rethought my decision about running into the race for this prestigious seat, but I had served and brought my region to incredible heights volume-wise. My efforts generated millions of dollars in profit for the company as I took my district from last place to first in a relatively short period. I ran an incredibly lucrative region with markets in Chicago, Denver, and Boston. Now, I was running the whole damn national firm. Suddenly and immediately, I found myself sitting in a boardroom in Irvine, California, contemplating preservation, another word for consolidation.

I was also three months pregnant, a surprise timing-wise, and not a perfect time to have the most significant task of my life coincide with the biggest job of my life to that point. I remember retreating to my car in the parking lot to cry. I cried because I had spent a decade building the firm, and now, I had the task of tearing it apart. I was broken inside about it, fueled by estrogen and a huge heart for the people I served. I returned to the boardroom, and somehow pulled myself together to the degree of being able to take the harsh consolidation orders I was given and carry out closures in Denver, Colorado, the first of the 14 major markets to fall. I trekked my pregnant self to their district, stood before 125 people, and laid them off.

I recall a man in the audience who had come to the company only weeks prior. He spoke up loudly in dismay, saying he had other choices and how this affected his family and his newborn child at home. I stood firmly in their strife and answered their heartache for hours. When, task completed, I carried my tired self to my room, I laid myself on a bed, and cried long into the night before returning home the next morning.

Soon after this I repeated the process three more times in other markets until one day, the real iceberg of our industry, the mortgage implosion era, became glaringly visible, and my firm had decisions to make. With a Fortune 500 stature and shareholder price at stake, they wanted answers from me about how we could ultimately save the situation. We were 60 percent of the size we once were and still not small enough to survive.

After sitting with the numbers for many days like a magician trying to pull a rabbit out of my hat, I could not find the mathematic equation to add up correctly without being in the red at the end of the day. The call to action I recommended was complete closure, which meant putting an end to a decade-long era of building and growth and putting myself out of a job in the process.

The pain I endured during this process was insurmountable. The gravity of hurt I felt for every human I had come to know, thousands of people who followed my leadership, and who worked tirelessly over the prior decade was immense. I felt as though we ultimately failed.

Years after this traumatic career intersection, I understood going through this tumultuous time was how I earned my true executive leadership wings. Until you lead in down-turned markets, you have not yet experienced leadership. Until you have had to give hope during hard times, give continued strength during bad markets, keep folks focused, and at work with a winning mindset despite taking on losses, you don't know the depths of leadership.

A month after I announced the complete closure of our beloved company, my mother fell ill to a brain aneurysm and spent several months recovering. She was in a forced coma for the first month. I slept on the waiting room floor then, and I know if I had not been out of work, I would not have been able to do that.

I also spent a summer with my new baby and wrote my first book, *Wise Eyes: See Your Way to Success*, a testament to the prior two decades' work in sales, captured while still fresh and given in tactical lessons.

My empath tweaking, which has throughout my life led to great focus, provided many gifts during this dreadful time, and the silver lining shone brightly, although I did not see it clearly then. What else can I call the time spent with my family and child and my writings but a gift?

My relationship with pain, in reflection, was one of raw feelings. The memories are vivid of how helpless I felt, unable to help the people who lost their employment. I understood what it meant to each family's security. It was the opposite of everything I had ever done. I knew I was removing the means of security for them and doing it when other jobs were not available in the industry.

Still, I believe I was the best man for the job. I did my work with great care; I spent countless hours soothing hurt souls. I sat with HR reps whom we retrained from onboarding to help create resumes and do off-boarding work which was some solace and assistance for these hurt people.

More than a decade later, I went through excruciating pain leaving AnnieMac Home Mortgage. Never did I know serving people and the bond of leadership could be so strong, and parting ways to begin the next chapter in my career would feel like I had abandoned all of them. I left caring tremendously for those people and peeling my white-knuckled hands off the steering wheel, fearing the sales division would feel neglected.

For days, weeks, and months I worried about the people, wondering who was taking care of what. I was haunted by worry until I eventually came to terms with the greater calling I now live in.

This calling had been pulling me towards where I am today for years. I knew there was more work to be done at a vaster level, and I could no longer sit in a company and not be able to spread my wings into the vast greatness and depth of the industry I serve.

Nobody saw my leaving coming which made it even harder. I had known in my heart for years; my time would come to an end there. I felt a pull away from my loyal place with them, and as if a spouse leaving an unaware mate, I was in a place I no longer felt I belonged.

My walk from leadership proved I am a servant leader and awakened me to how I serve and have served. It also taught me valuable lessons about the dangers of investing too much of myself in someone else's cause.

I lost myself over the prior decade when I gave all to a place; invested all my time and energy. They had been the benefactors of my divorce hurt; pain that acted like nitrous in an engine already soaring. I leaned into work with time and energy to survive with the pain of my lost marriage. In hindsight, that job saved me from another fall into depression or at least kept my nose above the waterline.

The techniques I learned to cope with the relationship to pain are mighty. I sat in professional counseling talking about my pain privately and coaching with Jay. Talking about this allowed me to tie two strings together. First, I recognized extreme emotion brought on by external factors causes pain.

Any of life's external hardships could bring me down. Learning these techniques changed my relationship with pain and put me in control.

To be clear, stuffing pain is not the answer. For most of my life, mine was an all-or-nothing mentality, either stand in pain and deal with it, or run and flee from it and never deal with it. When I chose the latter, I gave it more power to rear its ugly head and take me down at a later date.

Today, I control my pain with many careful processes. I have outlined below an action sequence I follow to move through pain, confront pain, and overcome pain.

### 1. RECOGNIZE YOU ARE IN PAIN THAT IS NOT GOING AWAY.

We can feel hurt often, but we need to recognize the difference when emotional pain unpacks its belongings intending to stay. Rate your pain, using the scale shown earlier in this chapter, to first understand WHO you are in relationship to pain.

## 2. COMPARTMENTALIZE THE PAIN.

I am not a doctor. I am the Einstein of pain, though, I promise you.

Having been the patient of trained counselors for three decades and having survived myself, I know we can wear pain like our skin and not shake it or we can wear pain like a pair of shoes and put them on the shelf when we want to go out dancing. I mean this logistically speaking, of course.

THIS WORKS! I have shared this trick with many others, and they have circled back to thank me. Today as I write this, I am in this methodology brought on by a sick sister. It is so heavy to face it, and yet I must daily. I wear the pain shoes as long as I have to, then I place them on a shelf.

## 3. USE THE ENERGY FOR POSITIVE THINGS.

I have fueled my entire life with pain. The product you see of my life is the result of not wanting to take the shoes off the shelf of pain so deep I could not sit with it. I innately stayed at my desk or stayed busy in life because I enjoyed the feeling, energy, and lift I received from being creative and working hard. Most of all, I coped by serving others as if pain was a proverbial cup to fill.

I used pain to drown myself in sorrow. I have let pain keep me down. You need to understand how mighty the urge is to give into pain. I have succumbed to it many days and weeks of my life leaving me lifeless in bed unable to do anything joyful; it was all consuming. I know reading this may be difficult for people to comprehend. I promise you: YOU CAN DO THIS!

## 4. SEEK PROFESSIONAL HELP.

I have been adequately raising my hand for two decades. I recall the first time I visited a doctor for my mental pain I left thinking I was not helped even as I sank to the depths of depression requiring in-hospital care due to weight loss and dehydration. I was in my late twenties when I woke up to my pain relationship. I sought and received help from a local mental wellness center. Not ideal for someone with an ego like me, who had to walk into this tall building in the downtown metropolitan city and pass through the homeless people standing in line or the droves of other sick people. But I didn't look at it through a lens of ego, I looked at it through a lens of desperation and heartache, knowing I was no different than the souls I passed in the hallways. Sure, my clothing may have been nicer, my purse some fancy brand name, but the person I passed covered in dirt and ragged clothes was simply further down a road I walked.

We forget people aren't born in this place; it is the place they end up when they can't save themselves. They are in survival mode, and the pain they feel no doubt is beyond anything we could bear.

If you studied how humans interact with seemingly sick people they relegate to loser status, we would see a deeply embedded stigma.

This is off-topic, but when you see a homeless person pandering, I know it's a huge decision to walk by without looking, never mind offering a dollar in their hat.

What about giving them the dignity of a good word? I am not saying to stand and talk, rather to not ignore them. THAT could change their day, their week and their life.

As I write this, my father is serving part-time as a landscaper for our local town. He is in charge of the parks. Recently, I walked the dogs with my dad, and we ran into some homeless people. He knew their names and their stories. It impressed me, yet didn't surprise me one bit. My father, my greatest teacher along with my mother, have always valued respect and dignity for all people regardless of their financial stature.

## 5. GET HONEST.

Living with kind and caring parents has always shown me a possible path and helped me walk through the doors of my doctor's office. For two decades I did the good work to unpack a lifetime of learning and unlearning. Choosing professional development on top of mental counseling allowed me to combine both parts of my life for the better.

I am a changed person because of it, for the better. I have more self-awareness than ever.

My next words are harsh but necessary. People are, by and large unaware of themselves. People think they know themselves, but they only know who they think they are. Not who they really are.

You will need someone who loves you to say, look at yourself, look at what you can't see, and what you blindly do not allow yourself to see. It requires a level of honesty I promise most people never reach. It is glaring to me when I see people in deep denial of the bad traits they possess. Depending on the gravity of each situation, I will attempt to be their person. I have been that person for many people over the years.

## 6. BECOME A HEALER

Learn through life's challenges, circumstances, and shaping.

I have become a healer. Not because I say so, but because those who are in my life tell me it is so. I take this on with great responsibility which has helped me take on more than I ever thought possible.

One might relate a healer to those in the Bible who did so with no riches and do not understand how a modern woman in 2022 can run a business, be wealthy, and be a healer. In truth, I came to this AFTER my wealth was developed. Interestingly, I have let go of the things I once desired from a material standpoint and have put my money into places like my new retreat home which is where I will do amazing work with those I love and those who desire to seek me out for work they want to do.

I am a healer. And I am healing people.

*CHAPTER 19*

# The Healer

Labels aren't always assigned appropriately. People decide about people and share inept insight, and suddenly the world is viewing someone wrongly. I have a relationship with labels that was, for most of my youth, a painful one. I lived in a trailer park which is considered unsavory by many standards. In truth, I lived in a warm, loving, and extremely clean environment, rich with moral fiber and family involvement. I lived amongst good, hard-working people. But I was nonetheless labeled.

Each of us hold within ourselves a code of ethics; our personal set of rules. Have you read the Bible? I have read parts but not its entirety. The message of this good book is lost on many. For those who profess faith in God or Jesus Christ, the Bible is a rule book and because of this notion many will not follow. Freedom is what they desire from the chains of rules and the rule makers.

The book of any religion relays the words and lays out the rules as interpreted by humans. We as people go through a phase of rebellion seeking autonomy from the rule setters. And often, when testing how to color outside the lines, we feel a certain euphoria, like a drug of its own sort. There can be a sense of excitement, making us feel alive. I know because I ran from rules most of my life. I would veer back into my lane and come across the proverbial finish lines, having driven the course and back roads the way I saw fit, more to control the narrative of the drive than to fall in line with the masses driving strictly on the course laid out.

Why people seek control and desire freedom is not a mystery. We are wired as I pointed out in the beginning a certain way which includes a thrill coming from living in a heightened sense of excitement. But it also kills us. I am not saying people who seek control and freedom are sinners, necessarily. I am saying many are unaware, like I was, how dangerous chasing can be, and how the chosen path goes against a long-written code.

Faith is an interesting subject to speak of and I would be remiss if in writing a book about finding honor I did not answer a deeply seated question about my personal faith or my beliefs for others in seeking a religious faith.

Before you think I am about to jump onto a pulpit and defend the word of God, I ask you to approach this part of the book with an open mind. Philosophically speaking and even scientifically speaking, the words written in the Bible are stories revealing a moral code, we all know. THAT code is internally wired in our human DNA. When we veer from the code, the choice will either raise us up or tear us down.

If one page had been added in front of the Bible where it warned the reader against veering from this course, explaining the choice would actually kill you slowly but surely, would anyone have read it with any more understanding and conviction? I don't really know. Rule followers may have taken it more seriously. Rule followers may be the people who are the most faithful.

Most of us are introduced to religion at a young age and most of us start going to church with our parents. Not everyone I realize; some people are introduced to faith by a spouse as an adult or a loving friend. I had my introduction by my parents as far back as my memory goes. We went to church often, although not consistently, every Sunday. We went to the significant holiday sermons. I recall standing in line for my red tissue-wrapped toy in the basement of the church where they had their giving time in celebration of the Christian holiday. I was always excited, and appreciative. It marked the holiday, and it also was meaningful because things came hard to our family. Growing up, we weren't showered with weekly gifts in my home. When we received something, we worked terribly hard for it. My parents always gave us incredible holiday Christmas's. They were hearty stock and mill workers and yes, they wanted my sisters and me to have faith in God and its principles.

In life, I veered far from the code learned as a child, but I never forgot the code existed. I veered far from the right and wrong I was taught but I never forgot what was right. Now I know the installation of these principles by parents is more important than making their children believe them fully or adhere to them fully because once the GPS is permanently installed, we will pull to and from its track accordingly, and we will go to and from things also the same way.

I wonder now and have spent the past few years contemplating a lifetime of suffering various labels, including those of being high feelings.

Being recently labeled a Healer is a label I am embracing and hope to grow into. I am encouraged to inspect and appreciate the good I have done with the challenges life has given me in translating what many consider a deficit to a superpower.

The Bible was not intended to be a story once read and put aside. The Bible is an ancient writing of the same code today and people are either veering from or adhering to it. People are becoming sick from their sins and are being saved from their wrongdoing by committing themselves again to that code.

I am someone who doesn't go to church regularly. I did however put my son through Catholic school upbringing all the way to middle school after which he moved into the public school system. The code I hoped to have him adopt I can see HAS been installed. I am less concerned about holding him strictly accountable to the code as I am pleased to see he veers to and from the code by his own doing.

When I think now about the long years I spent as a child with lack or lesser, I know now God was giving me a golden experience which once stripped, proved to be situational in as much as I have a deep relationship with impoverished people. I also know I was not poor by ethical standards; in fact, we were incredibly rich. I can see it clearly now. Our set of living standards was high; much higher than many of our wealthy neighbors.

I know now when I lost love in my life, both by my own doing or by others, God was teaching me how to overcome incredible pain. I know the same to be true about the addictions I have overcome in my lifetime. I quit smoking after 32 adult years.

About seven years ago, I was a pack-a-day smoker. One day just like that with no plan whatsoever I made a conscious decision to stop and never pick it up again. I had tried quitting many times over my lifetime and couldn't. I tried many types of assistance programs and all failed because I was not ready to receive the change. When you are ready, take the first difficult step and just do it. There is no in-depth guide to change, only a person's ability to put their faith in betterment by taking one step.

I see people all the time who can't and won't take step one sit on the sidelines of their lives thinking of the needed change and never take one step. I have taken the first step dozens of times in my life towards a more meaningful existence. Hard but worthwhile.

Over the past three adult decades, I can look back and see, even in the most difficult times, I administered my leadership and lessons to others. I was a perpetual student of life, and as soon as I learned something, I taught it. I made haste to share what I learned, whether a practical and tactical lesson within the realm of my professional world or something more meaningful like life lessons. And when times called for tough love or tough calls, I made them.

I have also learned people, however harsh our combined realities might be, by and large come back to my table. I am warmed by the thought of hard lessons administered and completed in a human and caring way, allowing people to resurface in my life. Even some I had to terminate in past lives impressed me by their ability to see me as a guide and not a dictator.

Over the years I dove far more deeply in assisting people. Seeing the suffering happening, I reached through barriers within my industry to serve with my firm. I have installed consultation services which address grief and wellness in a way I am certain none of my competition does. I do this because of human needs. As much as people need to sharpen the blade of their trade, they must pick up their swords to fight for themselves AND THAT is the greatest challenge of all.

I see how lost people are, and I help them get back on the path. I know when they are lost beyond their words or actions. Sometimes their words and actions tell me their obvious story; sometimes, it is more elusive. Sometimes it's completely hidden, but still, I see.

Do I think I have a superpower? No. I think I am powerful though. I think belief and faith are powerful, and I now know today my belief in people is my superpower. I know it's a gift of extraordinary power. I have seen what it does to propel change. I have seen what it does to save people.

I sat often with my dying sister over the past several years. This is not a statement I make lightly. Three years ago, her doctor gave her months to live. Her health was on a steep decline. She plummeted to the depths while living on full oxygen and entering assisted living care. She has rebounded many times with her health, but the decline always pulls her back; she is nearly down all the way.

We are only a few years apart in age, yet she is feeble and walks with a cane. She is sick and reaches out to me daily to listen. Her pain is palpable, and I pray for her not to suffer. Whatever is needed, I am available to help her, and sometimes, like today as I write this, I know my greatest job will be to go put on the shoes of pain and face her, to take her if she is able, for a car ride so the wind and sun can blow in her hair and shine on her face. My job is to sit with her, give her belief in her fight, and help her find her value and purpose in this life before it ends.

I know my job in this instance is one where I can't save her. I am not magical. But in healing her internally, will I prepare her for what's coming, the ultimate end? I believe I will. In helping her to heal, will I help my parents, my siblings, her child, and even myself? I think so.

Healing is not about something you see in a movie where I place my hand on the crippled person and suddenly, they are standing. I am not that kind of healer although I am certain those powers do exist in the world.

The kind of healing I do is mental. It is internal and, in the place most intimate in a person's world: their mind.

Today I have come to wear the label of a healer with great responsibility. I know I have the power to help a person when given the time and their intention is to become someone greater than they are. I do not think I know all. But what I know can make a difference; I am certain of it.

I have given long thought to the ultimate guide in life. A part of my life where I was suffering has turned a real corner, where I will take the lessons God gave me and ultimately spend my final days and years administering lessons to others to save them.

I am then nearing the end of my walk. While I know my walk could take me several more decades, if it is in my cards to be here on earth for so long, I realize I have developed into a healing human, and as a healer, this development is for all time.

I am a healer of the mind, it is a realization I will not squander. I do believe I need to concentrate on this power and give it time, energy, and respect. I know my days ahead will be filled much like a nun or a pastor or a prophet on a mission.

I will further study the great prophets and philosophers. We are building a library in my new retreat home; Jay is helping me by providing the list for the first 200 books. I have books coming to my doorstep weekly, all written by the greats; I am committed to having a relationship with these books for teaching. They will be available to the visitors who come to my home, and I will do incredible work with their knowledge. I desire the next level of my journey. I am still, as they say, on a journey of magnificent levels. I cannot wait to see what the next chapter brings me, knowing my duty and obligation in today's world. I am ready for this leg of the trip, down this long road of life.

CHAPTER 20

# The Journey

If you went on a vacation and afterwards someone asked you to survey the trip you would probably only do so if you were absolutely thrilled with it or absolutely dismayed. We are fickle humans who give our sentiments in the extreme realms of our thinking. Indifference is not a motivating place to be. Indifference is the place you end up when you stop caring.

Fortunately for me, when I look back today at my 52 years, I realize I have been living on both opposing ends of the emotional realm my entire life. I have either been soaring or completely falling down.

The third realm I have lived in is correcting. I have been correcting course for a good part of my life as I swung between the extremes.

## INDIFFERENCE

How many of you are living in the center of your lives and are feeling indifferent? I don't mean age wise but rather in the middle of the emotional realm of life where the extremes are not felt daily. You are not hurting nor are you elated and jovial. You are not dying nor are you soaring. You are existing.

What if I could urge you to reach beyond where you are? What if I could evoke a kind of emotion you would use to push out of your comfort zone and beyond? What would your then look like?

Have you ever wondered why children do unimaginable bad things knowing the rules of your home and leave you perplexed with their stupidity or their crass defiance? They are telling you something far deeper than the flour poured on the floor. They desire your attention. Internally, they are saying they need you.

I am not speaking of little toddlers or the undeveloped minds of babies; I am speaking of the more developed child in grade school who knows right from wrong to a varying degree but still knows. This is a child acting out and screaming for your attention. Such behavior is a sign to be taken seriously and to consider the depths of why. These opportunities to teach and learn come to alarm us and awaken us so we may see the neon lights of other souls.

All around us are lessons. We sit daily in the shock and awe of tragedy we witness on the nightly news. We see the world suffering. We see natural disasters taking out whole towns of people and we ask ourselves why? Sometimes we ask God why. We desire the answers. The events happening beyond our own imagination are incredibly difficult to answer and I am not going to pretend to have all the world's answers in this book.

I can tell you in my life's journey I have decided everything has meaning. When something sticks with me for days in the news, I think about why I am being stripped back this week in emotion. Why is this sadness here to visit? I have come to understand it's not for me to ask why but rather how. How do I turn the effects of my emotion into something positive? I realize the effect I experience is likely happening to others, especially in a global event.

Now, I turn my attention to see how to help others. My intuition even is like a spidey sense going off to an invisible threat. As discussed in the first chapter, my intuition has extraordinary power and laser exactness.

Once in recent years, during the pandemic, I was called to act. I realized within the first few days of the global pandemic confining us to our homes in an international worldwide lockdown, the suffering was at an extraordinary and incredibly deep level. The news filled us with scary images of barren streets and stories of those wrought with illness. It seemed the Armageddon we imagined had arrived. I wondered if I would ever see such an unbelievable plight and here it was.

## HOPE

I remember standing at the sink in my bathroom on day three with tears streaming down my face in fear of the situation. The gravity of it seemed impossible to face. Yet, I quickly wiped my tears away and knew from this day forward I would bring a word of hope to all who would come to the Zoom video classrooms I held. I would look back at the fear each day and assure them we would be OK.

Did I know for certain? No. But did I know we needed hope? Yes. Hope would soothe people greatly. Hope was incredibly necessary and powerful at that time, and providing the fuel of hope would perpetuate from my classrooms to the individuals' homes. It would ripple from their homes to classrooms, workplaces, and more. Soon enough, other leaders were doing the same, and although there were few of us speaking up and showing up in those initial days, we held court across huge geographical space with our messages.

The power of hope and belief is almighty. I am proud to administer it. It's a product of human life we all desire. It is not easy to find, I have come to realize, and not always naturally manufactured. I am a dealer of hope and belief, not for the paid for person but in trade of your time and your focus. If you give me both of those things, I will give you the ultimate power.

During the final writings of this book, I visited the place where I received hope: my elementary grade school. I wanted to enter a little democratic race for student council president and didn't sign up because of fear and insecurity. My school principal noticed and encouraged me. I entered the race and won.

This story is told in the opening chapter of *Wise Eyes-See Your Way to Success* and is credited as the moment I learned other people's belief in you could change your life. Mimicking this lesson as I have done with all great knowledge in my life, I became a teacher at the ripe age of 10 years old.

Imagine the power we each possess to change the world if we could collectively unite. Imagine the power you have as you read this book to change yourself and those around you. I have known my whole life I had this power but I have veered greatly from this path during my life.

When added up, all the years I either lacked, was sick or heart broken, my life has not been easy; there are more years spent in the depths of suffering than those spent happy, light, and benign. The balance is changing. The happier years are stacking now, and it seems I have finally broken the wild horse inside of myself and am running a pace of life safely. That is not to say I am any less driven than I ever have been because I have discovered my drive is an eternal candle.

## CORRECTING COURSE

There are too many stories of suffering and too many years of ruin to write in this book. My initial years from leaving home were harsh at best, and yet a lifetime ago. While seeking secondary education which was incredibly difficult and became fully reliant upon scholarship, I lived with a high school boyfriend in another state away from home. To protect him, because he corrected his own path many decades later, I will only say I lived a harsh few years in and around addiction. These years were exactly the kind of place a parent fears their child ending up in straight out of the home. I literally sprang into my life's dream and put myself directly on the path of destruction. Today I know the characters who surrounded me were in a similar plight, unknowingly trudging down a dead-end road in the dark. They too were innocent and young and simply misguided. I have fond memories entwined with sad ones, but I was completely thrown off my path in life because of not properly examining my situation and because of my bullheadedness to leave home and be on my own.

Moving out of that situation and beyond took incredible hardship and courage. I was young and it meant leaving everything I had known since I left home. It meant addressing my own ailments at the time. It meant leaving someone I truly loved. It meant leaving an entire community of established friends and work. It meant starting over.

It meant choosing to correct my course rather than simply accepting the road I was on. It would have been so easy to let the course play itself out. It would have been easier to accept

I had made a bad choice and live in it. Many people make this choice in life. I see it every day. They are in a relationship they are unwilling to leave due to the upheaval of their lives is too much to deal with or confront.

## FACING CONFLICT

Conflict is a mighty deterrent towards betterment. People see it as a flame flickering, one they will not burn themselves with. I, too, veered from confrontation most of my life because, frankly, it felt bad and left me almost always with guilt. I know now it was a trauma emotion for me triggered when I needed to stand in the uphill fight of debate. I spent many years avoiding it, and I know people I counsel today who have spent a lifetime themselves avoiding it.

The price of avoidance is a life sentence of not moving beyond where they sit or stand. The price of avoiding conflict has been expensive for most people. Relationships have stayed in hurtful places. Jobs have driven people to coping with solutions like drugs and alcohol. Familial strife has gone unanswered, causing breakdowns and complete severing of relationships. Children had been allowed to run astray out of avoidance of conflict or discipline. The cost of avoiding conflict is the most expensive emotional defect there is.

I did not know my relationship with conflict was bad, or figure this out on my own. I led myself back to the correct path to stand and deal with conflict with an almighty defense, and it was not natural for me.

Jay taught me about standing in conflict and together we peeled back the onion layers of its positive effects.

- Processing the Pain. When you stand in conflict and deal with the issue and move past it, you resolve internal pain.

- Confidence Boosting. A personal ability to stand in conflict is esteem-building and it helps you believe in the fights you are willing to make if your barometer is aligned with the TRUTH. If you fight for honesty, integrity, or the like, you will have shown up as a savior of a bad situation and help bring that situation to a positive place.

- Resolving/Resolution. Problems left unfixed break things. Eventually, when problems, emotions of a negative effect, and bad situations are left unfixed, this will break a relationship, company, or person. You can't resolve without standing in conflict.

## PROTECTING YOUR LIFE

Knowing this today and being an avid believer in standing in conflict, I can resolve daily the issues coming in to rob my company, my life, and my peace.

Today, having a huge life, I can see the issues others carry or bring to my table. When accidental evil came into my past life, I sat in those bad places for years when I made poor accidental choices. When bad situations came, I often gave in to them and one simple misstep would lead to years of wrong roads for me. Today it won't happen because of my self-awareness, my external awareness, and my ability to stand and deal with conflict.

I will not say it can't happen as I have learned never to say never, ever, forever, and always. Those are the words of dramatic, unseasoned, and unwise people. Those words are a mirage used to create dramatic expressions but are not actual words. I hear them today used by the unknowing, yet they are telling me, as if a beacon of light, warning you are dealing with an inept, emotionally aware person. I hear them loudly and stand in conflict with them almost always when I hear them.

## SAVE YOURSELF

Can a person die from sadness? I think so. I believe in my life I have been dying at times inside. The physical effects of depression are devastating when they impact choices and decisions that rip you apart limb to limb. Eating, drinking, consumption, activity, and relational work effects are damning in depression. The unrealized compound effects start a spiral hard to stop if not noticed or left unattended.

How do you stop yourself from dying of bad emotion? The first step is to be aware. Start with your health first.

- Diet. Are you eating a healthy and balanced diet? Would you be willing to change your diet today if it meant starting to take back control of your depression?

- Exercise. Would you do anything today to be active, even if it meant simply walking and getting up and moving.

- What are you putting into your body besides food? The answers here are diverse and extensive. Self-medicating is a deterrent to improved health. Seventy-five percent of drug and alcohol addictions begin with a desire to numb the feelings that are not dealt with properly.

- Correction here requires two fronts as I outlined in my chapter Escape Artist. If you need to go re-read it, please do. You must first address the addiction and then address the underlying emotion. This process, for me, took over a decade. The battle I fought took me years to correct. I am now living beyond those years.

- Relationships. Who is seated at your table? Who you spend time with and choose to spend time with is vital for your mental health. Run with the wolf pack you desire to elevate you. That is the tribe you need to find.

- Work. Your work can fulfill you or kill you. You can be indifferent and unemotional and simply see it as a means to an end financially. But if you are living in the soar-or-die realm of your work, you must ask yourself if you are in the right place. I have written whole books about my work and *Win or Learn* opens with a chapter called *Call me Crazy*. If you want to read about escaping from a job I was dying in, read that chapter.

I wrote another book called *Breaking the Cycle*. This book takes you on the journey of change and with a very encouraging tone teaches you many facets and evolutions of change. I have spent my entire life dedicated to the work and the lessons I know saved my life and corrected my course. I exist today knowing this is my purpose.

My journey has been a long road and I can't say it has been consistently happy. I can, however, say it's been consistently rich. Since my oldest memory, my life has been filled with love and excitement. My life has been in perpetual states of fight or flight. I have found the miles beyond the most trudged paths many of my friends have perished on. I have found my way beyond the hardship road to reach the road only open to the privilege of age and wisdom.

I am a teacher. I am a healer. I am a lover. This is who I have always been and always will be. Living in these traits and acknowledging my purpose and power has become my fight for a life mission. Today I live to help put these concepts into the world and see if I can spark incredible change beyond my wildest dreams.

I am living in my wildest dreams.

*CHAPTER 21*

# Finding Honor

How many times have I put my faith in an invisible God, a power or imaginary person or thing while praying for help and guidance in my life? All of my life.

When I didn't have the answers to this magic, I lived thinking bad things were just happening to me. I could not see my own hand in my demise in any situation. I never knew I was to blame for most of it.

To every person I have ever done wrong by, I apologize. Truly. I now know my part in my failures. I spent a fair amount of my life denying my own wrongdoing. I pointed to the external things as the reasons why. I defended bad actions and pointed to the causes, all of which were not my fault.

Today I understand bad luck, bad things, and bad situations usually occur from bad choices, bad decisions, and bad relationships.

## WHAT IS HONOR?

Honor is self-worth and self-value. Do you have it? I didn't for most of my life, but I didn't know. For many years, I thought I was great. Look at me, I thought. See my trophies and awards. Sure, I knew I could prevail in sales. I could win sales contests which is a huge part of the lessons I tactically teach today. I derive incredible confidence from my business abilities, and I see this in work I do for others, as well. However, solely allowing skills and accolades to be fuel for self-worth is damning. Awards and trophies can't make you love yourself, not fully anyways.

I didn't know my childhood fundamentally broke me until I did the work beyond rehabilitation. I didn't know for many years how the diagnosis I received of living in high emotion would steer so much of my living and decisions. I was attracted to the flame, and I was also attracted to the burn. Both.

When I spent time beyond the surface of my emotion, looking at it like a patient on a table with my certified counselor, as if an outside-of-body examination, I could see it easily. I had been chasing external approval brought on by some deficit I felt since a child. And this is probably an entire book for another time. I realized I didn't feel fully loved as a child. I did not feel I was worthy of love for some odd reason, whether rightful or innate, and whether by cause and effect or simply a cavernous void I could not fill, I realized the source of much of my pain. Examining why I felt this way was work spanning years and I found the underlying issues and truths about my inner wiring. Those truths unlocked the root cause, and it was then I could begin to understand and address the internal, deeply set issues plaguing me for a lifetime.

The damages prior to this discovery were staggering. I ran from healthy and strong relationships to feed something insatiable. I am grateful beyond words to no longer be running. And thank God because I am an old lady now. LOL! In all seriousness though, I am relieved and today secure in my self-love.

Honor would not come from this discovery alone, though. On top of discovering the root cause I also had to learn what those root causes affected in the behavior realm. I had picked up bad habits along the way. When you are covering up for a bad internal deficit you are often masking with many habits and practices which, in and of themselves, will deter you and your relationships. I had no idea how off-putting some of my traits were.

Today I cringe looking back at parts of my life. Although I can always see I meant well, and I can see good I did my entire life still. At my core was a beautiful barometer waiting to be calibrated. This, then, brings me to the paramount point of this entire book. Finding Honor! It was not simple or easy. But let me encourage you to put in the work. And let me inspire you as to why you should.

Jay and I had every reason to not have healthy relationships with life or each other or even our respective spouses and families. We had every reason to remain broken and lost. We found each other down a broken road alone and in need of discovery. I don't think it's an accident I saw Jay lecture publicly on The Liar Lid as one of our first encounters. I think it was exactly the message God needed me to hear at that time. Interestingly, I don't mind sharing with you the message was lost on many in the audience. I know it was above most people's level. I am about to enter a realm of intelligence in this part of the book where I hope you will really concentrate on hearing so you can walk away with the big aha moment here.

Finding Honor will only happen if you truly strip back the decades of your behaviors, examine them, and then commit to a set of conditions you yourself choose. I did this after correcting course, curing myself of repeated habits, quitting all addictive vices and dedicating myself to a healthy life, giving up sinful actions including gossiping and lying. And working beyond toward the purpose of my God-given life: giving hope and healing.

Today I am walking in honor and self-love. I am aligned and my moral barometer is calibrated. I know I am not perfect, and I am not seeking perfection. The confidence I have and the character building which occurred as a result is a feeling I have dreamed of feeling. I would never know this feeling had I not put in the work. I would not know pure happiness. PURE HAPPINESS!!

This is a fuel few ever feel because happiness is given out freely in dozens of varieties, many of which are derived from sinful initiations. Yes, we mistake pleasure for happiness, lust for happiness, material objects and the like for happiness.

PURE HAPPINESS can only come from a fuel available when you are beyond any level of elation ever before experienced. It burns purely and freely and endlessly with no fear of running out when it is brought on by living a life void of sin. Your internal wiring is calling upon you to find it. Everything we are made up of is only supposed to operate and work at its highest level when we find this path and way of living. Until then, we live in an altered and lesser state. I promise you it's a worthy journey.

What can you commit yourself to today to adjust your moral compass? What can you give up or set down to begin the journey of alignment? Would you put the work in if you could? Would you do the hard work to figure out how to self-love and cure the root cause of your problems first? Would you have the strength then to start on the rest of your behaviors? Would you be strong enough to unlearn bad habits and set boundaries around behaviors allowing you to live an honest life, to speak only the truth and to stand in the conflict that comes to you and work through it and past it? Would you then protect that living with your very existence? I know you can.

Allow me to put hope and faith in you right now as you read this. I have shared my most intimate details of my life. In doing so, I protected characters who may have played bad roles in my story not out of a lie or omission but rather out of the mere fact that this is my telling of my own story and not theirs. I have given enough depth in telling my story for you to know I am speaking a truth never before spoken in writing or out loud.

The writing of this book is a continuance of my journey to truth. I find myself telling stories I didn't know I would or could share. I have shocked myself in talking about my rehabilitation. I thought I would keep that bone buried for a lifetime, and then in my journey to truth and in finding honor, I realized there is no honor in not sharing a deeply rooted demise as a lesson for others.

I know my story will be TMI for some. There will be those who will find themselves changed. There will be others who have looked up to me and will change their view of who I am. There will be others who knew all along I live with this dark side of my life, and could see it a million miles away.

It is my hope in telling these truths you will be inspired by my courage, and I will be driven with more conviction to follow and pursue this road of honor I find myself on.

One of the effects of finding honor has been a brutal truth I speak today. As harsh as this is for all who surround my life, I can no longer look at other people's lies and denials with a blind eye. I have come to tell you the unspoken truth about yourself so if you sit with me know I can hear your lies and more often than not I will call those out in the right setting.

One of the other effects of my finding honor is I am lighter than a feather. I don't get heavy with guilt or shame easily. Do I make mistakes? Yes. I have made many mistakes still. Although the gravity is far less harsh, I misstep from time to time. My honesty is truly too much for some settings and I can look the antagonist as a result. In modern day and societal situations, my truth is too harsh for people. I know this to be true and I live with the knowledge of it. I try to pick my battles and read the room, all at the same time. It is not necessary every day or every moment to unleash the honest truth to everyone. There is a time and place where honesty is most effective.

An additional effect of finding honor is I am attractive to those seeking true betterment and a repellent of those who are fraudulent for true growth. People who are not willing to dive beyond the surface of their problems find me deep, and while I don't bring these things up over casual dinner settings, I am a beacon of light so bright I think many find themselves unable or unprepared to sit in my presence.

Another effect is I now think with abundance. I do not look at my competition or anyone else thinking they are coming to take from me or wondering how their success will hurt my own. I love the quote I once saw that says, "Blowing out another man's candle will not make your own shine brighter." How true I now know this is.

Finding honor rid me of jealousy. I once operated from an extremely jealous place both internally and with external relationships, both intimate and social. Today I am void of jealousy. I view success in others and relationships with my loves and friends as a gift for their happiness. My true happiness has made me willing to want this for others. As if my final acts on this earth will be to mimic this greatest lesson ever learned as I did my first lesson back in grade school. I now want to help others find honor.

Still, I attract the weary and downtrodden. I look around and people living this way with wealth and the unlikely success of great businesses operating efficiently and magnificently on a surface level. Many are broken internally and unsatisfied with their lives like my own, where the road of my ever-present success met my ultimate decline. I knew the only way I could truly believe the life my son would read about in the future when I had perished needed to be a real life lived with honor. I pursued it then with great urgency knowing if I died tomorrow, I would have lived an integral and decent life.

Finding honor and taking the journey to truth was a new realm of living I never even knew existed. Today, every room I am in is invigorating. Every ride I take on the weekend on my Harley Davidson with my life partner, Cory Parker, is soul inspiring. I see the trees and smell the winds of nature, feel the sun on my skin and I am light inside. I am thinking, what a beautiful life I am living. For many years this was not the case. I was missing my past life and felt responsible for not putting the pieces of it back together. I was in a life sentence and the heaviness would not lift. Today my ex-lives only a few towns away. He is remarried and while I have mourned the loss of our love, I have not tried to replace it or fill the void with another. I have come to terms with our love having to repair and evolve from its once original existence. I do love him still as the father of my child. I am happy for his found happiness with his new love, and she is magnificent and loving to my child. The plague I felt driving me into my deepest of depressions has been repaired and dealt with. I have forgiven myself. Let me repeat that. I have found the key and unlocked the door to the jail I threw myself in.

In what self-relegated prison are you living? Can you forgive yourself? Will you do the work? Can you live beyond your deepest sorrows and mistakes? Can you elevate your existence to a new place where you live as you know you were constructed to live rather than how you choose to live?

In finding honor, you will set yourself on a course towards unparalleled and the purest happiness ever felt if you can call upon the eternal wiring you have been born with. You can find your rules and adhere to them only through discovery and hard work.

Finding honor doesn't need to come as hard for you as it has for me. You may be inches away from your breakthrough. I obviously needed to come a long way back from a deterred path. I admit, in gratitude, this is not true for everyone.

Today I have fallen in love with my own flaws. I look in the mirror and I see my age. I accept myself as imperfect and I accept others freely as well. I do not judge today unless I see evil. I love and accept love at a higher level.

**REPURPOSED PAIN.**

I have repurposed my pain. There is so much I did with it. I used to think all the years I lay depressed, and all the years I lay in turmoil were a huge waste. Today I know the energy of those years is back in the universe. I have created a world where my work aligns with my purpose, and where I have endless energy to give and help others.

I have come to learn there are two kinds of pain. Guilty pain and pure pain. Guilty pain comes from evil or sinful actions. Pure pain comes from natural causes. We will NOT escape pure pain in our lifetime. In life, death and destruction will come and are not of our doing. We will need to deal with it when it comes, and we can do so in an integral manner.

Today I move through pure pain because of techniques I have shared in this book which allow me to compartmentalize pain and give it the focus and time it deserves while not allowing it to destroy me.

I avoid guilty pain today like it's the plague and I have very little of it. If you have regular pain brought on by guilt from a negative source like sin or evil, you must move yourself out of that place and change the course you are on, especially if this is a recurring daily theme. You are dying right now of that pain, and you don't even see its effects.

In ending this beautiful book and the writings of my journey I leave you with my final thoughts.

*CHAPTER 22*

# The Final Word

Just as Les Brown said in his foreword, "There is greatness in all of us." You will never know what your greatness is if heavier woes veil it. You will never unlock and hence unleash your power into a universe both thirsty and dying for your power unless you do the good work to find your own honor.

Beyond the realm of which you are living lies this incredibly pure happiness. You may be close or far away from it right now as you set down this book. For me I found honor because the internal light inside of me was calling me to it. Everything I felt in my high feelings state told me loudly when I did wrong and when I did right. I could not have eventually avoided it had I tried.

My superpower is giving hope and my purpose is providing belief to people all around me who need to know the God we must pray to is inside of each of us. The wiring to do incredible work and incredible things is here inside of us. We will not be finding it externally in any way, shape, or form, in its purest form, or with its most unfathomable power unless we turn inward, and do the work to unleash it.

Find your honor. Pursue your truth. The world is waiting for you to discover it.

# In Memorium

*In Loving Memory of Tammy Marie Trefrey, my older sister.*

Shortly after finishing *Finding Honor*, which she knew I was
writing, my sister passed
from her long battle with
many illnesses. In the
final month of her life, my
sister fought to die with
honor and accomplished
that in spades. She was
brave enough to live in her
pain and get up to be present every day, spending time with
family and friends. She made phone calls and wrote notes,
made amends, and tidied up her life in such a way we were

left knowing she was ready to pass on. Her sweetness and life-long pure gentleness were ever present in the final days of her life. Tammy's humor remained strong, and her dreams were hopeful and vivid, despite her knowledge she would soon be called to the Lord. She made an honorable departure from this world which is all any of us can ask for.

The presence of this example of living with honor seems omnipresent at the time I am writing this, a handful of days past her death. Tammy validates everything I wrote about fighting to find your honor. She was the living and best example of what this book represents.

Being where I was for the last two years writing this book allowed me to live in a place where I became the rock for Tammy. I spent much of the first two weeks after my sister passed lamenting what I  could have done, what I didn't do, and experiencing painful revelations.

It was while proofreading this book I realized with great clarity how the decisions I made in recent years helped me be her teacher in finding honor. The path this past year towards honor was not easy for her or for me. I almost can't believe I wrote this book on the precipice of the greatest loss of my life, talking about pain as if I knew the greatest level when still I did not.

In re-reading *Finding Honor* I was given a fresh view of tactics I needed in this moment of deep pain and hurt. I reflected on the mission I was on with my sister and realized

I did good work with her, and I gave her an incredible gift by helping her find her self-love and honor before the bitter end.

I was strong during our walk, although I was coping with great subconscious pain. The irony is strong in this; my greatest pain led me back to the words I wrote for others and helped me regain my footing to understand the scope and significance of the work she and I had done.

*Finding Honor* is truly a life's testament my sister vetted for the readers of this book. And if she can find it while dying, while fighting for her life, so can you. If she can do that, then I can save myself by remembering these lessons as well. Nothing is a coincidence to me in all of this. I think this is evidence of the hand of God working in real time.

God rest my sister's soul, and may she know she was and will always be my best friend in life. I will honor her for the rest of my days.

# ABOUT THE AUTHOR

Christine Beckwith

Award-winning best-selling author and founder of 20/20
Vision for Success Coaching, Christine Beckwith is a prominent
leader in finance. This groundbreaking entrepreneur believes
in paying it forward and taking action.

In all of Christine books she speaks of returning home, no longer on the other side of the tracks, per se. An early dream was to own a big home on the mountain side of her home town overlooking Lake Winnipesaukee. Twenty twenty-two saw the fulfillment of this dream. An unexpected bonus to accomplishing the dream was the joy Christine took in writing most of this book in her dream home overlooking the lake.

As is true of many dreams, the lake house has provided fruition of another of Christine's dreams, the development of 20/20 Vision's Retreat and Excursions division, created to provide self-development retreats in the years to come on the topic of *Finding Honor – The Journey to Truth*.

Made in United States
North Haven, CT
11 October 2022

25308326R00114